# THE LITTLE BOOK OF

# FASHION LAW

## URSULA FURI-PERRY

AMERICAN BAR ASSOCIATION
Defending Liberty
Pursuing Justice

Cover design by Mary Anne Kulchawik/ABA Design.

Printed in the United States of America.

27 26 25 24 23   6 5

**Library of Congress Cataloging-in-Publication data is on file.**

**ISBN:** 978-1-62722-111-5

# Table of Contents

# Introduction

## What Is Fashion Law?

The field of fashion and beauty law is new. It is exciting. It is anything but boring.

Susan Scafidi, professor and academic director at the Fashion Law Institute at Fordham University School of Law, explains:

So what is fashion law, exactly?

It is a field that embraces the legal substance of style, including the issues that might arise throughout the life of a garment, starting with the designer's original idea and continuing all the way to the consumer's closet. As a course, we defined fashion law to include four basic pillars: intellectual property; business and finance, with subcategories ranging from employment law to real estate; international trade and government regulation, including questions of safety and sustainability; and consumer culture and civil rights. In addition to its central focus on apparel and accessories, fashion law includes related areas such as textile production, modeling, media, and the beauty and fragrance industries.

From a practice perspective, fashion law can include the representation of clients engaged in the design, manufacturing, distribution, or retail sectors, among others, or even of consumers. While many of these stakeholders are part of an elaborate global system and work closely together, requiring an emphasis on licensing and other transactional work, others are structurally at odds with one another. For example, the interests of domestic manufacturers and importers often differ, as do the perspectives of creative designers and fast-fashion copyists. This complicates the policymaking process for the fashion industry, which is far from monolithic. Of course, as with all legal fields, fashion law requires swords as well as plowshares, and the fashion industry sees its fair share of litigation.[1]

Lawyers who practice fashion law might find themselves handling many different issues and questions from various practice areas and facets of the law. Just consider the following examples:

- The lawyer might be asked to help protect a fashion law client's intellectual property, such as trademarking the client's logo or filing a patent application on a particular garment feature that the client invented.
- The lawyer might be asked to go after an infringing party who is close copying the client's new line of dresses.
- The lawyer might need to draft licensing agreements on behalf of a client who wants to license a new line of accessories to other companies.
- The lawyer might draft vendor agreements or retailer agreements on behalf of a client who wants to get a line of perfumes into independent stores.
- The lawyer might draft import-export agreements with foreign parties or be asked to research relevant laws regarding importing or exporting garments.
- The lawyer might assist the client with obtaining financing and draft up relevant documents.
- The lawyer might research various governmental regulations, including consumer safety issues and environmental laws.
- The lawyer might assist with employment agreements, non-compete agreements, or freelance contracts for designers, models, or other parties whom the client wants to employ.

---

1.    Susan Scafidi, *Fiat Fashion Law! The Launch of a Label—And a New Branch of Law, in* NAVIGATING FASHION LAW: LEADING LAWYERS ON EXPLORING THE TRENDS, CASES, AND STRATEGIES OF FASHION LAW (2012).

- The client might ask the lawyer to help with an employment discrimination claim.
- The lawyer might draft commercial real estate documents or assist with real estate transactions.
- The lawyer might assist with a merger or acquisition.

These are just a few examples of hypothetical issues that lawyers who practice in this new and unique field might find. Of course, because fashion law is new, the evolution and history of fashion law is likewise interesting.

Alan Behr, partner and head of the fashion and luxury goods practice at Alston & Bird LLP, writes:

Fashion law is a relatively new area of legal practice. At the beginning of the twentieth century, the fashion industry was predominately a highly fragmented, East Coast concern. Few clients employed general counsel, and few budgeted significant legal expense to protect their rights. The business was very competitive, marked by relatively low margins of profit, with precious little allocated to professional services. The fashion market was easily accessible with very low capital requirements, but frustratingly difficult to penetrate. Investment was confined to very tangible needs, rarely available to support legal work other than basic organizational formation, including the choice of business organization and location, compliance with basic and very limited regulatory issues, occasional labor or union problems, minor intellectual property work, and the legal necessities occasioned by exiting from the business.

Much has changed in the fashion industry since the end of World War II to require more highly developed legal skills, and, happily, to demand a much greater allocation to legal expense. The industry is hardly confined to one region; it is entirely global, and the gritty nature of fashion commerce is now somewhat obscured by unremitting glamour depicted in every type of media. While still fragmented, a surprisingly large number of members of the fashion industry have grown into mega-multi-nationals, with large in-house legal departments and brand name law firms to match the power of their own brand names. These companies have become enormously powerful and media savvy, and they are capable of penetrating any market directly, through print, and via the Internet. To be sure, the vast number of fashion businesses only aspire to reach the heights of the numerous public and private fashion giants, with stables of trademarks, worldwide licenses, branded retail locations, and close working relationships with the great retailers of the world, but in that aspiration, fashion industry members have to resort to legal assistance to build a proper aspirational foundation.[2]

---

2. Alan Behr, *In Fashion Law, Timing is Everything, in* NAVIGATING FASHION LAW: LEADING LAWYERS ON EXPLORING THE TRENDS, CASES, AND STRATEGIES OF FASHION LAW (2012).

# THE LITTLE BOOK OF

# FASHION LAW

# Fashion Law and Intellectual Property

*"Fashions fade; style is eternal."*

**— YVES SAINT-LAURENT**

# Chapter One

# In The Beginning, There Was Piracy

*Millinery Creators' Guild, Inc. v.*
*Federal Trade Commission*, 109 F.2d 175
(2d Cir. 1940).

*Fashion Originators' Guild of America, Inc.*
*v. Federal Trade Commission*, 312 U.S. 457
(1941).

*WM. Filene's Sons Co. v. Fashion Originators'*
*Guild of America*, 90 F.2d 556 (1st Cir. 1937).

Piracy, when applied to the law of intellectual property, is "a generic term for the infringement of a copyright or patent through counterfeiting or duplication."[1] Piracy cases present a unique dichotomy in court: the quest to protect intellectual property while ensuring compliance with antitrust laws and allowing free competition to blossom.

Pirates are not just on the high seas—they are also part of high fashion. The fashion industry has long dealt with the issue of piracy, and early court decisions reflect the prevalence of the problem.

In the 1940 case of *Millinery Creators' Guild, Inc. v. Federal Trade Commission*, the Second Circuit Court of Appeals decided

---

1. *Privacy, in* BOUVIER LAW DICTIONARY 809 (Stephen M. Sheppard ed., 2011).

an important issue: may a fashion trade association seek to restrain competition by putting self-regulating controls upon designs?

Millinery Creators' Guild was a trade association organized (at least in great part) with the purpose of combating the practice of "style piracy." By pursuing "cooperation agreements" with retailers, setting minimum prices, and establishing a "registration bureau" for designs by its members, the Guild sought to limit competition. Members of the Guild agreed not to sell women's hats to stores that purchased from pirates, and retailers agreed not to buy any hats that were pirated designs of registered members' hats.[2]

The court noted that the Guild's "concerted action to eliminate style piracy extends beyond the permissible area of industrial self-regulation"[3] and extends instead into the area of impermissible restraints on competition.

"The purpose of the milliners, and the necessary effect of their combination, is to maintain their price structure, and to eliminate a distasteful 'evil' which the law nevertheless recognizes to be a socially desirable form of competition," the court stated. "Such an antithesis is unavoidable: what is desirable competition to the consumer may be outlaw traffic to the established manufacturer. But while we maintain the competitive system, a monopoly in an idea, not recognized by positive law, must be jealously scrutinized lest the few are protected at the expense of the many."[4]

The following year, in *Fashion Originators' Guild of America, Inc. v. Federal Trade Commission*, the United States Supreme Court addressed a cease-and-desist decree by the Federal Trade Commission (FTC), which prohibited textile and garment makers

---

2. *Millinery Creators' Guild, Inc. v. Federal Trade Commission*, 109 F.2d 175 (2d Cir. 1940).

3. *Id.* at 178.

4. *Id.*

from practices that constituted unfair competition.[5] In that case, textile manufacturers, garment manufacturers, and their affiliates adopted a scheme under which textiles were to be sold to garment manufacturers only on the condition that buyers would not use or deal in textiles that had been copied from manufacturers' designs. Another condition stipulated that the retailers would not use or deal in copied garment designs.

The court ruled against the textile and garment makers in the *Fashion Originators'* case. The Supreme Court held that even if systematic copying of dress designs constituted a tort, that situation would not justify dress manufacturers in combining to regulate and restrain interstate commerce in violation of federal law for the purpose of combating the evils growing from the pirating of original designs.[6]

"In this case, the Commission found that the combination exercised sufficient control and power in the women's garments and textile businesses 'to exclude from the industry those manufacturers and distributors who do not conform to the rules and regulations of said respondents, and thus tend to create in themselves a monopoly in the said industries,'" noted the Supreme Court. "While a conspiracy to fix prices is illegal, an intent to increase prices is not an ever-present essential of conduct amounting to a violation of the policy of the Sherman and Clayton Acts; a monopoly contrary to their policies can exist even though a combination may temporarily or even permanently reduce the price of the articles manufactured or sold."[7]

In an even earlier case from 1937, however, the fashion industry found a more friendly decision in the First Circuit Court of

---

5. *Fashion Originators' Guild of America, Inc. v. Federal Trade Commission,* 312 U.S. 457 (1941).

6. *Id.* at 468.

7. *Id.* at 467.

Appeals. Filene's operated a ready-to-wear specialty store in Boston, with numerous branches in other parts of Massachusetts. In 1933, Filene's entered into an agreement with the Fashion Originators' Guild of America, whereby retailers would agree not to buy or sell "pirated" styles and designs, and whereby designers who belonged to the Guild would agree not to engage in style or design piracy, also registering their designs with the Guild. Retailers who refused to cooperate, or were discovered not to cooperate, were "red-carded" by the Guild, and members were told not to provide those retailers with any designs or manufactured fashions. In 1936, Filene's repudiated its contract with the Guild, upon which it was red-carded and lost some of its suppliers.[8]

Filene's sued and lost in the district court. The appeals court affirmed, holding that the Sherman Antitrust Act did not necessarily preclude the members of an industry from collectively acting to eliminate "evils" and establish fair competitive practices. [9] "The mere fact that a contract or combination regulates or imposes some restraint upon the trade in interstate commerce does not necessarily make it illegal," the court held.[10]

The court did refer to the FTC's decision (already in place) in the matter of *Millinery Guild*, but differentiated it from the *Filene's* case. The court noted that Filene's had a reasonably adequate market outside of the Guild and that any loss in revenue was not accomplished through fault of the Guild. [11] "[T]he facts found by the Trade Commission are quite different from those found by the master and adopted by the [d]istrict [c]ourt in the case at bar. In the matter of the Millinery Guild the Commission found that the

---

8. *WM. Filene's Sons Co. v. Fashion Originators' Guild of America*, 90 F. 2d 556 (1st Cir. 1937).
9. *Id.* at 561–562.
10. *Id.* at 561.
11. *Id.* at 562.

Guild formed a substantial majority of the originators of the leading style of high-grade millinery for women. The master found the
facts otherwise in the case at bar. The Commission found that the
plan of the Millinery Guild, its acts and practices were to hinder
competition and to create a monopoly in the sale of women's hats
in interstate commerce by increasing the price and limiting production to the injury and prejudice of the public, while the master
in the case at bar found to the contrary."[12]

In a much earlier case, the Second Circuit Court of Appeals
declined to offer protection to a silk manufacturer that put out
new designs and patterns each season. In *Cheney Bros. v. Doris
Silk Corporation*, the plaintiff silk manufacturer sued the defendant, which allegedly copied one of the plaintiff's designs and
undercut its prices. The court noted that most of the plaintiff's
patterns were seasonal, only lasting for a short while, and many
of the patterns did not "catch the public fancy."[13]

The court held that Cheney Bros.' seasonal designs did not warrant protection. "It is in practice impossible, and it would be very
onerous if it were not, to secure design patents upon all of these;
it would also be impossible to know in advance which would sell
well, and patent only those. Besides, it is probable that for the
most part they have no such originality as would support a design
patent," the court noted.[14]

---

12. *Id.*
13. *Cheney Bros. v. Doris Silk Corporation*, 35 F. 2d 279 (2d Cir. 1929).
14. *Id.* at 279.

# Fashion Law Fact:

With the American Civil War came the introduction of mass-produced, ready-to-wear clothing for men—a real change from the past, when most clothing was custom made to order. Women's clothing continued to be custom made until the 1920s and 1930s, which saw the development of improved mass production techniques, chain stores, and mail-order catalogs.[15]

---

15. *A History of Standard Clothing Sizes: How Sizes Developed and Why the Same Size Does Not Always Fit*, Fᴀꜱʜɪᴏɴ Lᴀᴡ Wɪᴋɪ, http://fashionlawwiki.pbworks.com/w/page/11611137/A%20History%20of%20Standard%20Clothing%20Sizes%3A%20How%20sizes%20developed%20and%20why%20the%20same%20size%20does%20not%20always%20fit (last visited May 22, 2013)

# Chapter Two

# Fashion Law and Intellectual Property:

## The Road to the IDPPPA

*Abercrombie & Fitch Stores, Inc. v. American Eagle Outfitters, Inc.*, 280 F.3d 619 (6th Cir. 2002).

To protect intellectual property, there are generally several means available.

- Trademarks: A trademark is "any word, name, symbol, or device or any combination thereof used by a person, or which a person has a bona fide intention to use in commerce and applies to register . . . to identify and distinguish his or her goods, including a unique product, from those manufactured or sold by others and to indicate the source of the good, even if that source is unknown."[1]A service mark is "a word, phrase, symbol, and/or design that identifies and distinguishes the source of a service rather than goods."[2]

---

1. 15 U.S.C § 1127 (???? - year missing)
2. U.S. Patent and Trademark Office, *Trademark, Patent, or Copyright?*, USPTO. COM, http://www.uspto.gov/trademarks/basics/definitions.jsp (last visited May 22, 2013)

- Trade dress: Quoting from the landmark case of *Two Pesos, Inc. v. Taco Cabana, Inc.*, trade dress depicts "the total image of a product and may include features such as size, shape, color, or color combinations, texture, graphics, or even particular sales techniques."[3] A 2002 case saw a battle between rival retailers Abercrombie & Fitch (A & F) and American Eagle (AE), both of which cater to the young, hip, athletic crowd.[4] A & F sued AE, claiming the latter retailer infringed on A & F's trade dress in its clothing designs and its catalog configuration. Some of the "unique and inherently distinctive features" that A & F identified and argued were part of its trade dress included the use of words and phrases such as *performance, authentic, outdoor* and *genuine brand* in advertising and promotional materials; use of all natural cotton, wool, and twill fabrics and primary color combinations; and the creation of a cutting edge "cool" image through photos and advertising.[5]

As to clothing designs by A & F, the court declined to hold that those were protectable trade dress, as they were functional. "The aura about a product, the cachet that ownership or display of it creates, and the kind of appeal it has to certain customers does not dress a good in trade," the Court stated. [6] "Rather, those intangible 'things' emanate from the good, its dress, and the marketing campaign that promotes the dressed good. Trade dress is tangible or otherwise objectively observable by the senses; its constitution is a matter of subjective interpretation."[7]

---

3. *Two Pesos, Inc. v. Taco Cabana, Inc.*, 505 U.S. 763, 764 (1992).
4. *Abercrombie & Fitch Stores, Inc. v. American Eagle Outfitters, Inc.*, 280 F. 3d 619 (6th Cir. 2002).
5. *Id.* at 624–626.
6. *Id.* at 630–631.
7. *Id.* at 631.

However, the *Abercrombie* court held that the plaintiff's configuration of its retail catalog was, indeed, protectable trade dress. The court noted that trade dress has received expanded protection in recent years. It cited to McCarthy on Trademarks, section 8.4, to note that "trade dress has been held to include such things as the cover of a book, a magazine cover design, the use of a lighthouse as part of the design of a golf hole, the 'G' shape of a Gucci watch, a combination of features of a folding table, a fish-shaped cracker, the 'Marlboro Man' western cowboy motif, and, most notably for our purposes, the layout and appearance of a mail-order catalog."[8]

However, to A & F's loss, the court also held that while A & F's catalog was protectable, AE's catalog was not confusingly similar to the plaintiff's catalog—in other words, it did not infringe. Therefore, the court affirmed the lower court's grant of summary judgment for AE.

- Patents: According to the U.S. Patent and Trademark Office, a patent "is a limited duration property right relating to an invention, granted by the United States Patent and Trademark Office in exchange for public disclosure of the invention."[9]
- Copyrights: According to the U.S. Copyright Office, "[a] copyright notice is an identifier placed on copies of the work to inform the world of copyright ownership," and "[a]s a general matter, copyright infringement occurs when a copyrighted work is reproduced, distributed, performed, publicly displayed, or made into a derivative work without the permission of the copyright owner."[10]

---

8. *Id.*, at 630.

9. U.S. Patent and Trademark Office, *Trademark, Patent, or Copyright?*, USPTO. COM, http://www.uspto.gov/trademarks/basics/definitions.jsp (last visited May 22, 2013)

10. U.S. Copyright Office, *Definitions*, COPYRIGHT.GOV, http://www.copyright.gov/help/faq/faq-definitions.html (last visited May 22, 2013)

Unfortunately for legitimate fashion designers who want to protect their designs, "useful articles" are not protected under copyright law. A useful article is defined as "an article having an intrinsic utilitarian function that is not merely to portray the appearance of the article or to convey information."[11] Clothing is often considered to have quite utilitarian functions, which makes the applicability of copyright law difficult. In a Connecticut Law Review article, Meaghan Ehrhard explains: "Just as a painting is in reality simply paint on a canvas, and a work of literature is words on a page, what is produced through fashion design is an article of clothing. This functional aspect of fashion design is the primary reason why there is no copyright protection for such designs in the United States. This functionality also raises a problem of public choice for legislators: knockoffs in the clothing industry hold the unique position of being both productive and unproductive. Copying in the fashion industry decreases a designer's return on investment, creates barriers of entry into the design market, and distorts innovation. However, copyists also make high-end fashion designs accessible to the general population. As a result, when Congress debates the extension of copyright protection to fashion design, the argument inevitably devolves into a debate over the best situation in a Catch-22: should American law encourage and reward the innovators in the fashion design industry, or does society instead want to promote the 'democratization' of fashion?"[12]

Two forms of copying plague the fashion industry: interpretational copying and close copying. Arielle Cohen, in the Chicago-Kent Journal of Intellectual Property, explains: "Fast-fashion is the 'low-cost, high-scale, rapid copying' of original designs of

---

11. 17 U.S.C § 101

12. Meaghan McGurrin Ehrhard, *Protecting the Seasonal Arts: Fashion Design, Copyright Law, and the Viability of the Innovative Design Protection & Piracy Prevention Act*, 45 Conn. L. Rev. 285 (2012).

a lower quality at a discount price. The fast-fashion dilemma lies not in the interpretational copying of trends or styles but in the 'exact' or 'close copying' of original designs. The difference is that a close copy is a line-by-line copy of a design and looks almost if not exactly identical to the original design, while an interpretational copy is an original design itself that follows a current trend. Many large chain stores employ these fast-fashion methods of copying in order to capitalize on current fashion trends. . . . Designers oppose close copying because retailers profit from the designers' work while there is no economic benefit to the designer, which in turn, creates a disincentive for designers to create new designs."[13]

So, what's a legitimate designer to do? In a great effort to better protect fashion designs as intellectual property, a decades-long struggle has resulted in the introduction of the Innovative Design Protection and Piracy Prevention Act (IDPPPA), which has seen several incarnations as proposed bills in Congress. The new IDPPPA would propose to fit copyright protections for fashion design into the U.S. Code, specifically into chapter 13 of title 17, which was originally a copyright system created for boat hulls in 1998. It would define an "infringing article" as "any article the design of which has been copied from a design protected under this chapter, or from an image thereof, without the consent of the owner of the protected design. An infringing article is not an illustration or picture of a protected design in an advertisement, book, periodical, newspaper, photograph, broadcast, motion picture, or similar medium."[14]

The proposed IDPPPA goes on to state:

---

13. Arielle K. Cohen, *Designer Collaborations as a Solution to the Fat-Fashion Copyright Dilemma*, 11 Chi.-Kent J. Intell. Prop. 172, 173

14. Innovative Design Protection and Piracy Prevention Act, H.R. 2511, 112th Cong. (2011), *available at* http://thomas.loc.gov/cgi-bin/query/z?c112:H.R.2511:

In the case of a fashion design, a design shall not be deemed to have been copied from a protected design if that design—

(A) is not substantially identical in overall visual appearance to and as to the original elements of a protected design; or

(B) is the result of independent creation; and

(3) by adding at the end the following:

(h) Home Sewing Exception—

(1) IN GENERAL—It is not an infringement of the exclusive rights of a design owner for a person to produce a single copy of a protected design for personal use or for the use of an immediate family member, if that copy is not offered for sale or use in trade during the period of protection.[15]

The IDPPPA also lays out specific requirements for a cause of action against a potentially infringing design:

Pleading Requirement for Fashion Designs—

(1) IN GENERAL—In the case of a fashion design, a claimant in an action for infringement shall plead with particularity facts establishing that—

(A) the design of the claimant is a fashion design within the meaning of section 1301(a)(7) of this title and thus entitled to protection under this chapter;

(B) the design of the defendant infringes upon the protected design as described under section 1309(e); and

(C) the protected design or an image thereof was available in such location or locations, in such a manner, and for such duration that it can be reasonably inferred from the totality of the surrounding facts and circumstances that the defendant saw or otherwise had knowledge of the protected design."[16]

---

15. *Id.*
16. *Id.*

For many (if not most) fashion designers, the passage of the IDPPPA would be welcome. Ehrhard notes the main arguments for the bill's passage: "The IDPPPA is a viable solution toward overcoming these intellectual barriers that have historically blocked the extension of intellectual property protection to fashion design. It crafts a definition of protectable designs that can reconcile the competing interests of designers, retailers, and consumers. The IDPPPA also creates a cause of action for infringement against only blatant copyists, thus encouraging innovation and dissemination of trends. Furthermore, the IDPPPA's three-year window of protection is specifically tailored to the transitory lifetime of fashion design."[17]

Of course, there are cons to every pro. "[A]rguments for the passage of the IDPPPA are countered with the general assertion that copyists are a strong social equalizer. Copyists are able to quickly translate the designs of haute couture into cheaper fabrics for sale to the American masses through retail chains,"[18] Ehrhard writes. "Fashion designers have attempted to counter this fear with the assertion that designers do not seek protection in order to achieve isolation, but instead to gain the exclusive right 'to have the chance to knock off their own designs before others do it for them.' Designers argue that they would never earn a profit by selling their designs only to a select few. Instead, the main profit is accrued from affordable ready-to-wear lines based upon their high-end originals. Copyists prevent this natural business from evolving, however, since with copyright protection, 'the average consumer can wear affordable new designs created by true designers rather than poor copies of the real thing made by pirates in China.'"[19]

---

17. Ehrhard, *supra* note 29, at 288.
18. *Id.* at 305.
19. *Id.*

# Fashion Law Fact:

Sumptuary laws are defined as "laws made for the purpose of restraining luxury or extravagance, particularly against inordinate expenditures in the matter of apparel, food, furniture, etc."[20] American colonies such as Virginia and Massachusetts enacted sumptuary laws in the seventeenth century regarding the wearing of certain colors, styles and fabrics.

---

20. BLACK'S LAW DICTIONARY, 1436 (6th ed. 1999).

# Chapter Three

# Fashion Marks and the Lanham Act:

## Considering the "Likelihood of Confusion" in Fashion Handbags

*Louis Vuitton Malletier v. Burlington Coat Factory Warehouse Corp.*, 426 F.3d 532 (2d Cir. 2005).

*Louis Vuitton Malletier v. Dooney & Bourke, Inc.*, 454 F.3d 108 (2d Cir. 2006).

*Coach Leatherware Company, Inc. v. AnnTaylor, Inc.*, 933 F.2d 162 (2d Cir. 1991).

"The most important form of protection for fashions and accessories is the most commercially oriented one: trademark law. At its simplest, a trademark identifies the source of goods. For many companies in the business, however, especially those in the luxury sector, their trademarks are the most effective communication devices for the most enduring property that the brand has, which is its story."[1]

When consumers shell out big bucks for a brand-name luxury handbag, they expect to get certain things for their money: the use of quality materials, the practicality of the bag for its intended purposes, aesthetically pleasing looks, and of course, adherence to and prominence of the luxury brand for which the customer is paying. And when consumers purchase less expensive look-alikes, they presumably know better than to expect the same luxurious perks, but nevertheless hope to get a bag that in many ways resembles those manufactured by luxury firms. As the luxury bag business has flourished, so has the look-alike handbag business.

The "likelihood of confusion" in fashion handbags has been at the forefront in various cases involving popular luxury handbag manufacturers. In *Louis Vuitton Malletier v. Burlington Coat Factory Warehouse Corp.*, the United States Court of Appeals for the Second Circuit addressed this issue after luxury fashion design firm Louis Vuitton brought suit against discount clothing and accessory chain Burlington Coat Factory.[2]

The *Burlington Coat Factory* case involved Louis Vuitton's famed toile marks, the company's flagship designs, which were originally introduced in France in 1896, and the company's "Multicolore" marks, introduced in 2003 and developed by designer Marc Jacobs and artist Takashi Murakami. The court explained the great success of the Multicolore marks (which resemble the original toile marks, in an updated and colorful pattern), noting that

---

1. Richard Reinis, *An Exploration Into the Practice of Fashion Law, in* NAVIGATING FASHION LAW: LEADING LAWYERS ON EXPLORING THE TRENDS, CASES, AND STRATEGIES OF FASHION LAW (2012)

2. *Louis Vuitton Malletier v. Burlington Coat Factory Warehouse Corp.*, 426 F.3d 532 (2d Cir. 2005).

production of the handbags had not kept up with their demand; the opinion of the court also notes that, to the date of its release, sales of the Multicolore handbags totaled over $25 million.

At the center of contention was Burlington's line of beaded handbags, which the court described as having "colorful designs reminiscent of the LVM Multicolore bags,"[3] and the issue of whether Burlington's bags amounted to trademark infringement and counterfeiting, as alleged by Louis Vuitton, in violation of the Lanham Act.

The Lanham Act, first enacted in 1946, is the primary federal statute protecting against trademark infringement and dilution, along with false designations of origin and false descriptions.[4] One part, commonly known as section 43(a) of the act, provides for the filing of a civil action in cases of dilution or false designations of origin.[5]

## §1125. False designations of origin and false descriptions forbidden

a. **Civil action.**

   1. Any person who, on or in connection with any goods or services, or any container for goods, uses in commerce any word, term, name, symbol, or device, or any combination thereof, or any false designation of origin, false or misleading description of fact, or false or misleading representation of fact, which--

      A. is likely to cause confusion, or to cause mistake, or to deceive as to the affiliation, connection, or association of such person with another person, or as to the

---

3. *Id.* at 535.
4. Lanham (Trademark) Act 15 U.S.C. §§ 1051–1141
5. 15 U.S.C. § 1125(a)

origin, sponsorship, or approval of his or her goods, services, or commercial activities by another person, or

B. in commercial advertising or promotion, misrepresents the nature, characteristics, qualities, or geographic origin of his or her or another person's goods, services, or commercial activities, shall be liable in a civil action by any person who believes that he or she is or is likely to be damaged by such act.

To analyze the applicability of the Lanham Act, most courts will use the two-pronged test dealing with trademark infringement: First, the court will address whether the plaintiff's mark merits protection under the act. Second, the court will determine whether the defendant's use of a similar mark is likely to cause consumer confusion.[6]

In *Burlington Coat Factory*, the lower court's ruling ultimately favored Burlington. The district court concluded that when it came to the products, point-of-sale confusion by the customer was unlikely. Therefore, the court reasoned, Louis Vuitton had not established a sufficient probability of success on the merits, denying the company's request for an injunction.[7]

During the appellate *Burlington Coat Factory* case, however, the court emphasized that to determine whether two products are so similar as to promote confusion, it is improper to conduct a side-by-side comparison of the products. Rather, the court said emphasis should be on actual market conditions and the type of confusion alleged. The court noted that it is only a natural reaction

---

6. See *Gruner & Jahr USA Publishing v. Meredith Corporation*, 991 F.2d 1072 (2d Cir. 1993).

7. *Louis Vuitton Malletier v. Burlington Coat Factory Warehouse Corp.*, 426 F.3d 532, 536 (2d Cir. 2005).

to place two products next to each other when one is faced with a claim that the products are confusingly similar to consumers; however, the court also noted that where products in the market typically are not displayed in the same locations, the focus on such side-by-side comparisons is improper.[8]

In the end, the appellate court vacated the trial court's judgment and remanded the case for further proceedings. "On remand," the appellate court instructed, "the court should give particular weight to any evidence submitted by the parties addressing the overall impression that consumers are likely to have of the handbags when they are viewed sequentially, and in different settings, rather than simultaneously."[9]

In a later case, Louis Vuitton's trademark Multicolore handbag and toile marks were once again at the center of controversy. *Louis Vuitton Malletier v. Dooney & Bourke, Inc.* dealt with a similar trademark infringement claim, this time filed against handbag manufacturer Dooney & Bourke.[10]

The court in the *Dooney & Bourke* case noted the importance of taking handbag protection seriously—for purposes of practicality and fashion. "We cannot help but observe that for the person carrying it, a handbag may serve as a practical container of needed items, a fashion statement, or a reflection of its owner's personality; it may fairly be said that in many cases a handbag is so essential that its owner would be lost without it."[11]

The appellate court held that "the trial court made the same mistake that we criticized in Burlington Coat Factory: inappropriately focusing on the similarity of the marks in a side-by-side comparison instead of when viewed sequentially in the context of

---

8. *Id.* at 539.
9. *Id.*
10. *Louis Vuitton Malletier v. Dooney & Bourke, Inc.*, 454 F.3d 108 (2006).
11. *Id.* at 111.

the marketplace," and once again remanded the case and vacated it in part.[12]

But Louis Vuitton was not the first handbag designer to go to court to protect its trademark designs. The *Louis Vuitton* cases followed an earlier case involving famous "affordable luxury" manufacturer Coach. In *Coach Leatherware Company, Inc. v. AnnTaylor, Inc.*, the United States Court of Appeals for the Second Circuit addressed the issue of similarity in design—this time, centering on the use of tags in designer handbags.[13] As Coach claimed in its advertising slogan, "It's not a Coach bag without the Coach tag," so it claimed that AnnTaylor's use of tags in some of its handbags violated the copyright of the registered Coach tags.[14]

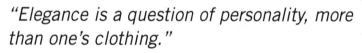

*"Elegance is a question of personality, more than one's clothing."*

— JEAN PAUL GAULTIER

At the lower level, the trial court had granted summary judgment for Coach, enjoining AnnTaylor from replicating any of Coach's handbag styles. The appellate court affirmed in part. Although the court held that Coach failed to establish that AnnTaylor violated

---

12. *Id.* at 117.
13. *Coach Leatherware Company, Inc. v. AnnTaylor, Inc.*, 933 F.2d 162 (2d Cir. 1991).
14. *Id.* at 168.

section 43(a) of the Lanham Act, it also upheld the decision for Coach based on section 32, which provides for the protection of registered marks. The court reasoned that "[u]nlike unregistered trade dress claims, disposition by summary judgment is often appropriate where the protection of a registered trademark is at issue."[15] AnnTaylor's tag, though it may have contained AnnTaylor's name, was confusingly similar to the look and feel of Coach's tag, thereby establishing likelihood of confusion under section 32.

In a much earlier case, the Second Circuit Court of Appeals addressed the issue of unfair competition as applied to handbags. In *Lewis v. Vendome Bags, Inc.*, the plaintiff was a manufacturer of handbags who sued another maker for copying the plaintiff's design, which was *not* embodied by a patent held by the plaintiff. The appeals court refused to discuss that issue, reversing the district court's order of an injunction and holding that the federal court lacked jurisdiction, as the designs were not covered by federal patent laws.[16]

Even if the court had jurisdiction, the decision went on to say, the plaintiff presented insufficient facts for a victory. "The plaintiff's name was stamped upon the lining of its bags; the defendant's bore no name. There are no findings, and no indication that there was any evidence, to the effect that the defendant palmed off its bags as the plaintiff's product, or that the design . . . had become so associated with the plaintiff in the mind of the public as to acquire a secondary meaning and cause any bag of the same appearance to be ascribed to the plaintiff as the source of production. . . . The essence of the wrong of unfair competition is selling the goods of one manufacturer or vendor as those of another, and unless

---

15. *Id.* at 170.
16. *Lewis v. Vendome Bags, Inc.*, 108 F.2d 16 (2d Cir. 1939).

the defendant passes off its goods as those of the plaintiff, the action fails."[17]

Some might say imitation is the highest form of flattery. In court, however, imitation can be costly. The next chapter looks at an ongoing case at the time of the writing of this book—a case that has one designer seeing red.

---

17. *Id.*

# Chapter Four

# Seeing Red:
## The Battle Over Your Sole

*Louboutin v. Yves Saint-Laurent*
(ongoing litigation).

Call it more than just a shoe. Call it a fashion statement, a
status symbol, a work of art, and a trademark design unto
itself. People would not say this about many shoes, but
some shoes do merit such a description, among them the famous
red-soled heels designed by Christian Louboutin.

Louboutin's heels are perhaps most famous for their red outsoles, a design that not only serves as Louboutin's trademark style
but is also actually protected by a federal trademark registration.
Thus, when competitor Yves Saint-Laurent (YSL) rolled out four
styles of monochromatic red shoes in its seasonal collection in
2011, Louboutin sought to enforce its trademark. It filed a suit
against YSL in the United States District Court for the Southern
District of New York, asserting various claims under the Lanham
Act and New York law and seeking a preliminary injunction to
prevent YSL and other competitors from being able to use red
outsoles (in particular, those painted the shade of "Chinese Red,"
the shade used by Louboutin).

33

As the district judge told it: "Whether inspired by a stroke of original genius or, as competitor YSL retorts, copied from King Louis XIV's red-heeled dancing shoes, or Dorothy's famous ruby slippers in 'The Wizard of Oz,' or other styles long available in the contemporary market—including those sold by YSL—Christian Louboutin deviated from industry custom. In his own words, this diversion was meant to give his line of shoes 'energy,' a purpose for which he chose a shade of red because he regarded it as 'engaging, flirtatious, memorable and the color of passion' as well as 'sexy.'"[1]

In its opinion, the court acknowledged that red outsoles have certainly become a mark associated with the plaintiff. In fact, the court observed, in branding the red sole, "Louboutin succeeded to the point where, in the high-stakes commercial markets and social circles in which these things matter a great deal, the red outsole became closely associated with Louboutin"[2] The court went on to cite the song "Louboutins" by Jennifer Lopez as an example.[3]

Nevertheless, the court concluded that despite the existing mark, which was granted to Louboutin, the red soles did not warrant protection under the Lanham Act. Trademark protection, the court observed, "applies to color not as an abstract concept, or to a specific single shade, but to the arrangement of different colors and thus their synergy to create a distinct recognizable image purposely intended to identify a source while at the same time serving as an expressive, ornamental or decorative concept."[4] So, while a distinct combination or pattern of color—such as a famed checkered pattern or a colorful monogram—would merit protection

---

1. Decision and Order at 2, *Louboutin v. Yves Saint-Laurent* (2011) (No. 1:11-cv-02381-VM).
2. *Id.* at 3.
3. *Id.*
4. *Id.* at 12.

under the Lanham Act, the court decided that the monocolor out-sole in question did not.

The court entertained a "fanciful hypothetical," involving the great artists Monet and Picasso. Suppose, the court indulged, that Picasso sought to enjoin Monet from selling or displaying works in which Monet used a specific shade of indigo, which Picasso claimed was the "color of melancholy," the hallmark of Picasso's Blue Period. Should Picasso's injunction be granted? The court answered no, proceeding to compare art to fashion by noting that both art and fashion are devoted to aesthetics and embrace matters of taste.[5] "Placing off limit signs on any given chromatic band by allowing one artist or designer to appropriate an entire shade and hang an ambiguous threatening cloud over a swath of other neighboring hues, thus delimiting zones where other imaginations may not veer or wander, would unduly hinder not just commerce and competition, but art as well."[6]

Next, the court addressed the question of the functionality doctrine, noting that the use of a single color has been held functional, and therefore not deserving of trademark protection under the Lanham Act. The court reasoned: "The outsole of a shoe is, almost literally, a pedestrian thing. Yet, coated in a bright and unexpected color, the outsole becomes decorative, an object of beauty. To attract, to reference, to stand out, to blend in, to beautify, to endow with sex appeal—all comprise nontrademark functions of color in fashion."[7]

In sum, the court held that Louboutin's claim should not be allowed lest it stifle competition in the fashion industry, "cast[ing] a red cloud over the whole industry, cramping what other designers

---

5. *Id.* at 13.
6. *Id.* at 17.
7. *Id.* at 20.

could do, while allowing Louboutin to paint with a full palette."[8] Louboutin's motion for preliminary injunction was denied on August 10, 2011.

Louboutin appealed the trial court's judgment on October 17, 2011 to the United States Court of Appeals for the Second Circuit. In its appellate brief, Louboutin argued three major points:

1. The district court erred in holding that the red outsole mark was not entitled to trademark protection on the ground of aesthetic functionality.
2. The district court erred in holding that a single color on a fashion item could not act as a trademark.
3. The court's denial of the preliminary injunction was an abuse of discretion, as the court's analysis was legally erroneous.

"Color as a trademark is provided for in the Lanham Act and has been upheld by the United States Supreme Court and by this [c]ourt in controlling precedent ignored by the [c]ourt below," the appellant's brief states.[9] The law will not accept a 'blanket prohibition' because '[w]hen a color serves as a mark, normally alternative colors will likely be available for similar use by others."[10]

In addition, Louboutin argued that the red outsole mark is a strong brand identifier (to the point where Louboutin spends about $2 million yearly on protecting its mark), that it is not impaired by the doctrine of functionality, as it is not essential to the manufacture or sale of women's high fashion designer shoes (in fact, it adds to the cost of manufacture), and that it has not impaired competition. "The court below recognized the distinctiveness and

---

8. *Id.* at 23.
9. Brief of Christian Louboutin S.A., at 20 *Louboutin v. Yves Saint-Laurent* (2011) (No. 1:11-cv-02381-VM).
10. *Id.* at 21.

fame of the Red Outsole Mark as an identifier of the *CHRISTIAN LOUBOUTIN* brand but improperly gave no weight to the statutory presumption of validity, engaged in an improper dissection analysis of the mark, grossly overstated the limitations imposed by the mark on competitors and ignored undisputed proof of likelihood of confusion and irreparable harm to Louboutin."[11]

In response, YSL filed its appellate brief on December 27, 2011. In it, YSL argued that Louboutin cannot overcome the "formidable hurdle" necessary to obtain reversal of the lower court's order.[12] In fact, YSL argued that the "better practice," as established by the circuit court, after denial of a preliminary injunction is to seek an expedited trial on the merits, rather than an interlocutory appeal as sought by Louboutin.[13] A trial on the merits, YSL noted, would allow the appellate court to engage in meaningful review.

YSL also argued that Louboutin was unlikely to overcome YSL's functionality defense, and therefore, the court did not abuse its discretion by denying the preliminary injunction below. "If a mark is functional, a plaintiff's trademark claims fail, even if the mark has secondary meaning and even if there is likelihood of confusion," the brief noted.[14] "[T]he color red has been used as an ornamental feature on the outsoles of footwear for decades (if not centuries),"[15] and YSL has used it on the outsoles of its shoes since the 1970s. In fact, YSL argued, Louboutin himself acknowledged that the use of the red outsole was first adopted to "give life to a creative concept," and not to establish a brand identifier.[16]

---

11. *Id.* at 22. (emphasis original)

12. Brief of Yves Saint-Laurent America Holding, Inc. at 15, *Louboutin v. Yves Saint-Laurent* (2011) (No. 1:11-cv-02381-VM).

13. *Id.* at 11.

14. *Id.* at 19.

15. *Id.* at 12.

16. *Id.*

Louboutin countered with a reply brief, filed on January 10, 2012. "Well-established principles of trademark law promote and reward innovation and fair competition in the marketplace and protect consumers from confusion about source and quality. Legitimate competitors avoid a lacquered red outsole. Imitators and copyists damage Louboutin's business by damaging the brand and violating public source identification."[17] Although the trial court never actually referred to "aesthetic functionality," Louboutin argued that by rejecting the red outsole mark due to design appeal, it effectively invalidated the mark on the basis of aesthetic functionality, which was a strictly limited doctrine.[18] Furthermore, Louboutin argued that YSL had failed to prove that it, or any other competitor, has suffered commercial restrictions arising from the enforcement of the mark. Footwear designers have a multitude of alternate shades to choose from to create—including, Louboutin pointed out, 100 or so other shades of red—and YSL must only refrain from using a shade of red that would serve to be confusingly similar to Louboutin's red outsole mark. "Louboutin asks for no more and is entitled to no less."[19]

In support of Louboutin, jewelry giant Tiffany & Co. filed an amicus curiae brief on October 24, 2011. Tiffany argued that the district court's per se rule that a single color for fashion items cannot be a valid mark was erroneous and should be rejected by the appellate court. (It is no surprise that Tiffany noted its interest in the case by explaining its use of the famous blue box in packaging its products, which it described as "so well known that consumers instantly associate it with Tiffany."[20])

---

17. Reply brief of Christian Louboutin S.A. at 1, *Louboutin v. Yves Saint-Laurent* (2011) (No. 1:11-cv-02381-VM).

18. *Id.* at 9.

19. *Id.* at 13.

20. Brief of Tiffany (NJ) LLC and Tiffany and Company as Amici Curiae Supporting Respondents at 2, *Louboutin v. Yves Saint-Laurent* (2011) (No. 1:11-cv-02381-VM).

"[W]hether a single color trademark is valid and legally protectable is a fact-intensive question that must be analyzed on a
case-by-case basis to examine, *inter alia*, whether the *particular* mark at issue is registered and whether the *particular* mark
has acquired secondary meaning among the relevant consuming
public, and thereby identifies a single source. There is not (and
there ought not be) a *per se* blanket rule in trademark law that
precludes single colors from being valid trademarks in the fashion industry (or any industry), and this [c]ourt should reject the
[d]istrict [c]ourt's adoption of such a sweeping rule."[21]

In September 2012, the appeals court released its decision, holding for Louboutin and reversing the decision in part. Discussing
the utilitarian functionality doctrine, the court noted: "Louboutin's trademark, consisting of a red, lacquered outsole on a high
fashion woman's shoe, has acquired limited 'secondary meaning'
as a distinctive symbol that identifies the Louboutin brand."[22] The
court did limit its decision to cases where the red outsole contrasts
with the color of the remainder of the shoe, however.[23] As a result,
because the original suit involved litigation over a monochromatic
shoe, Louboutin's injunction was denied.

Of course, this case was hardly the first one to address the copying of shoe designs. In *Eliya, Inc. v. Kohl's Department Stores*, the
plaintiff Eliya, Inc., a designer and manufacturer of shoes, sued
Kohl's Department Stores, alleging that Kohl's copied one of Eliya's shoe designs and sold the copied shoe at its retail stores. The
plaintiff alleged violation of various common law and statutory
prohibitions.

---

21. *Id.* at 13. (emphasis original)
22. See U.S. Court of Appeals for the Second Circuit at 2, *Louboutin v. Yves
Saint-Laurent* (2011) (No. 1:11-cv-02381-VM).
23. *Id.*

"Eliya clearly articulates the specific features of the shoe design that comprise its trade dress—the stitching patterns on the front and side of the shoe and the strap, the design of the strap itself, the labels, and the pattern on the wrap-around sole," the court noted. "The Federal Rules require only notice pleading, and Eliya's description of its trade dress is sufficient to provide Kohl's with sufficient notice regarding the features of the shoe design that Eliya alleges Kohl's has infringed."

Louboutin also was not the first landmark case to address the ability to trademark a single color. In fact, the appeals court in the *Louboutin* case cited at length to *Qualitex v. Jacobson Products, Inc.*, which previously held that the Lanham Act allows for a single color alone to meet the basic legal requirements for use as a trademark. In that case, the color in question dealt with a manufacturer's dry cleaning pads that were a particular shade of green-gold.[24]

The *Qualitex* court argued that color "can act as a symbol that distinguishes a firm's goods and identifies their source, without serving any other significant function. . . . The green-gold color acts as a symbol. Having developed secondary meaning (for customers identified the green-gold color as Qualitex's), it identifies the press pads' source. And, the green-gold color serves no other function."[25]

---

24. *Qualitex v. Jacobson Products, Inc.*, 514 U.S. 159 (1995).
25. *Id.* at 165.

# Fashion Law Fact:

According to the Return Fraud Survey conducted by the National Retail Foundation in 2008, over 64 percent of retailers have experienced "wardrobing," which refers to the consumers' practice of returning used, nondefective merchandise.[26]

---

26. National Retail Federation, *Retailers Adjusting Return Policies to Provide Good Customer Service in Down Economy*, NRF.COM, http://www.nrf.com/modules.php?name=News&op=viewlive&sp_id=600 (last visited May 22, 2013)

# Chapter Five

# Fabric Designs and Copyrights and Trademarks

*Eve of Milady v. Impression Bridal,*
957 F. Supp. 484 (S.D.N.Y. 1997).

*Lois Sportswear v. Levi Strauss & Co.,*
799 F.2d 867 (2d Cir. 1986).

*Wal-Mart Stores, Inc. v. Samara Bros.,*
529 U.S. 205 (2000).

I t is a firmly established rule in the courts that clothes, in their functional purpose, are not copyrightable. Fabric designs are, however, considered "writings" for the purposes of copyright law, and therefore merit protection.[1] This maxim was at the center of controversy in a federal case involving the lace designs of bridal dresses filed in the United States District Court for the Southern District of New York.

In *Eve of Milady v. Impression Bridal*, the plaintiffs, designers and sellers of bridal dresses and owners of copyrights in lace designs of bridal dresses, filed suit against the defendant for copyright infringement. Eve of Milady claimed that Impression Bridal,

---

1. *Eve of Milady v. Impression Bridal*, 957 F. Supp. 484, 489 (S.D.N.Y. 1997).

a Texas manufacturer and seller of bridal dresses, engaged in advertising and selling bridal dresses, the designs of which were strikingly similar to five of the designs offered by Eve of Milady. There is, as everyone knows, a difference between well-made clothing and poor imitation. Interestingly, in its summary of the facts, the court noted, "Milady contends that Impression has previously copied Milady dress styles. Milady took no action against Impression because it believed that these copies were of poor quality and thus posed no threat to Milady's interests."[2] The five designs in controversy, however, were different "[b]ecause defendants' dresses incorporate well-made copies of plaintiffs' designs, plaintiffs believe they will suffer serious harm to their reputation and business."[3]

The plaintiffs sought an injunction that would prohibit Impression Bridal from representing that their bridal dresses are plaintiffs' products or displaying or using plaintiffs' proprietary marks. They also sought to prohibit Impression from not only copying or manufacturing bridal dresses that were substantially similar to the plaintiffs' designs but also from filling any orders of such dresses; in fact, the plaintiffs requested that the court order Impression to contact its customers and recall all of Impression's bridal dresses. (Imagine being the bride who gets *that* call just before the wedding!)

The court applied a two-part test: First, the plaintiffs had to show that their work was actually copied by proving "access" by the defendants to the copyrighted work.[4] The court noted access was proven in this case by way of an advertisement placed by Eve of Milady in a bridal magazine, which allowed the defendants to

---

2. *Id.* at 488.
3. Id.
4. *Id.* at 487.

gain access to the lace designs.[5] Second, the plaintiffs had to show "improper" or "unlawful" appropriation of the copyrighted work.[6] Here, the plaintiffs met this burden as well; the court noted that similarities between the dresses extended to the designs of laces and their placement on the dresses.[7]

Ultimately, the court sided with Eve of Milady, granting the injunction, which prohibited Impression from copying or manufacturing bridal dresses that were substantially similar to the plaintiffs' designs, among other things. And as for that recall order? Well, the court reasoned that "[f]or consumers who have purchased dresses but have not yet been married, such an order would be a source of immediate prejudice to the brides who had planned to wear the defendants' dresses at their weddings."[8] Retail stores, however, are different; they can be enjoined without causing the same prejudice as the consumers would suffer.[9] The court, therefore, granted the plaintiffs' request with regard to filling orders made by retail stores.

Bridal wear is clearly special, but even everyday clothing deserves design protection in court. Consider the next case, which deals with a much more down-to-earth design: the stitching pattern on the back pockets of jeans.

*Lois Sportswear v. Levi Strauss & Co.* involved a dispute regarding the back-pocket stitching on Levi's jeans, a recognizable pattern of two intersecting arcs that bisected both jeans pockets, to which popular clothing manufacturer Levi Strauss held a federal trademark.[10] Lois Sportswear and Textiles Y Confecciones Europeas, the plaintiffs, were importers of luxury jeans, some of

---

5.  *Id.* at 489.
6.  *Id.* at 487.
7.  *Id.* at 490.
8.  *Id.* at 491.
9.  *Id.*
10. *Lois Sportswear v. Levi Strauss & Co.*, 799 F.2d 867 (2d Cir. 1986).

which had a back pocket stitching pattern "substantially similar" to Levi's jeans (the court, in fact, described it as "the two patterns are virtually identical when viewed from any appreciable distance.")[11]

As the court detailed, the two parties had clashed over the stitching pattern since 1979, when Levi Strauss filed a protest with the United States Customs Bureau regarding Lois Sportswear's and Textiles's importation of jeans, claiming that the imported jeans violated Levi Strauss's trademark rights, serving as grounds for barring further importation. At first, the Customs Service sided with Levi Strauss, banning the importation of the jeans in 1980, but it reversed its decision in 1981. A year after that, the Customs Service once again banned importation. In 1982, Lois Sportswear commenced a suit in the Court of International Trade against the Commissioner of Customs. In that case, the court issued a preliminary injunction against banning the importation of Lois Sportswear's jeans.[12]

In 1982, Lois Sportswear then sued Levi Strauss in federal district court, seeking a declaratory judgment that its use of the stitching pattern did not violate Levi Strauss's trademark rights. The defendant counterclaimed for damages and an injunction and later filed a separate action against Textiles. The two actions were consolidated, and the district court ultimately held for Levi Strauss.

In the appellate case, the court agreed, stressing that there was a likelihood of confusion as to the relationship between the parties due to the similar stitching patterns. "[T]he Lanham Act was designed to prevent a competitor from such bootstrapping of a trademark owner's goodwill by the use of a substantially similar mark," the court explained.[13] Lois Sportswear argued that there

---

11. *Id.* at 869.
12. *Id.* at 869.
13. *Id.* at 872.

was little likelihood of consumer confusion, as Lois dealt mostly in designer jeans, but Levi Strauss tended to manufacture more casual jeans. The court shot down that argument, reasoning that Levi Strauss had an interest in preserving its trademark should it decide to enter the designer jeans market and that consumers could reasonably assume that the jeans in question, associated with the popular Levi's stitching, were a sign of Levi Strauss's entry into the designer jeans market segment.[14] Furthermore, the court pointed out that "[i]n the post-sale context, this striking similarity no doubt will cause consumers to transfer the goodwill they feel for appellee to appellants, at least initially. This misuse of goodwill is at the heart of unfair competition."[15]

In another important case, Samara Brothers, Inc., a children's clothing designer and manufacturer, brought action against the mega-retailer Wal-Mart, which Samara claimed had sold knockoff copies of the designer's clothes, alleging infringement of unregistered trade dress.[16]

In 1995, Wal-Mart contracted with Judy-Philippine, Inc., a supplier, to supply Wal-Mart with a line of children's outfits for sale. Wal-Mart had sent the supplier a number of photos of garments from Samara's line, on which Judy-Philippine's garments were to be based. The supplier then copied, with only some minor changes, sixteen of Samara's garments. Many of the garments by Samara had contained copyrighted elements. In 1996, Wal-Mart stores carried and sold the copied lines, and it reportedly generated more than $1.15 million in gross profits.[17]

---

14. *Id.*, at 873.
15. *Id.* at 874.
16. *Wal-Mart Stores, Inc. v. Samara Bros.*, 529 U.S. 205 (2000).
17. *Id.* at 207–208.

The jury sided with Samara, and the district court denied Wal-Mart's motion for judgment as a matter of law. The appeals court affirmed.[18]

The Supreme Court, however, sided with Wal-Mart and reversed the Second Circuit's decision. "We hold that, in an action for infringement of unregistered trade dress under s[ection] 43(a) of the Lanham Act, a product's design is distinctive, and therefore protectible, only upon a showing of secondary meaning."[19]

The court went on to note that "design, like color, is not inherently distinctive. The attribution of inherent distinctiveness to certain categories of word marks and product packaging derives from the fact that the very purpose of attaching a particular word to a product, or encasing it in a distinctive packaging, is most often to identify the source of the product. Although the words and packaging can serve subsidiary functions—a suggestive word mark (such as "Tide" for laundry detergent), for instance, may invoke positive connotations in the consumer's mind, and a garish form of packaging (such as Tide's squat, brightly decorated plastic bottles for its liquid laundry detergent) may attract an otherwise indifferent consumer's attention on a crowded store shelf—their predominant function remains source identification. Consumers are therefore predisposed to regard those symbols as indication of the producer, which is why such symbols 'almost automatically tell a customer that they refer to a brand.'"[20]

---

18. *Id.* at 208.
19. *Id.* at 216.
20. *Id.* at 212.

# Fashion Law Fact:

The Fashion Law Institute, which is currently housed at Fordham Law School, was established in 2010 with help from the Council of Fashion Designers of America.[21]

---

21. Susan Scafidi, *Fiat Fashion Law! The Launch of a Label—And a New Branch of Law*, *in* NAVIGATING FASHION LAW: LEADING LAWYERS ON EXPLORING THE TRENDS, CASES, AND STRATEGIES OF FASHION LAW (2012).

# Chapter Six

# My Good Name Is Valuable! But to What Extent?

*Calvin Klein Trademark Trust v. Wachner,*
123 F. Supp. 2d 731 (S.D.N.Y. 2000).

L icensing of a particular trademark, copyright, or other intellectual property is an important facet of the law governing the world of fashion and beauty. Clearly, those who own a particular mark have a significant interest in ensuring that anyone who has a license to use that mark keeps the integrity of the product intact. As an example, a luxury clothing designer can seek to prohibit licensees from selling its products in discount stores. Should the licensee fail to comply, the designer might elect to sue the licensee for various claims—perhaps breach of contract, perhaps trademark or trade dress infringement. But does the licensee, trusted to use the designer's good name in an effort to keep its integrity, owe a special fiduciary duty to the licensor?

In *Calvin Klein Trademark Trust v. Wachner* a federal district court in New York said no.[1] The case involved Calvin Klein and the Calvin Klein Trademark Trust as plaintiffs, who filed suit

---

1. *Calvin Klein Trademark Trust v. Wachner*, 123 F. Supp. 2d 731 (S.D.N.Y. 2000).

against several licensees entrusted with the use of the CK marks on various women's intimate apparel, men's underwear, men's accessories, jeans, and jean-related items. Among the plaintiffs' beefs were a decision to sell certain items to JC Penney,[2] distributions of Calvin Klein products to discount stores, and sales of products at outlet stores.[3]

The court reasoned that the plaintiffs' allegations simply amounted to a breach of contract or a claim for trademark or trade dress infringement and that no provision of the Delaware Business Trust Act (on which the plaintiffs had relied) provided that beneficial owners of a business trust had further fiduciary obligations to each other.[4]

The court also didn't agree with plaintiffs that the customer suffered when designer products were sold at discount prices, which the plaintiffs claimed deceived customers into thinking that there was more CK sponsorship than there actually was.[5] "[T]o the extent that [the plaintiffs' complaint] alleges that consumers are likely to be misled into believing that CKI has agreed to the distribution of 'first quality' Calvin Klein goods at discount stores, it is hard to see how the consumer is harmed at all, rather than benefited, from believing that CKI approved the consumer's receiving first quality goods at rock bottom prices."[6]

---

2. *Id.* at 736.
3. *Id.* at 737.
4. *Id.* at 734.
5. *Id.* at 737.
6. *Id.*

# Chapter Seven

# What's in a (Trademarked) Name?

*V.E.W., Ltd. v. The Vera Co.*, 2007 WL 1370469 (S.D.N.Y.).

The plaintiff: Vera—Vera Wang, the designer, that is, through her companies V.E.W. Ltd. and V.E.W. Licensing, LLC

The defendant: also Vera—The Vera Company, LLC, which originated with the artist Vera Neumann, known for her bold and colorful pints and scarves and owned the "Vera" trademarks.[1]

The question: who may use the name Vera and in what capacity?

In 2007, after negotiating a deal with Kohl's to sell Vera Wang designs, the plaintiffs sought to use the newly proposed trademarks "Very Vera Vera Wang" and "Simply Vera Vera Wang." The problem? Someone else—namely, the defendant's company—was also using the trademarked name "Vera." The plaintiffs sued, seeking a declaratory judgment to allow them to use the newly proposed trademarks.[2]

The defendant filed a motion to dismiss the suit, claiming that the court lacked federal subject-matter jurisdiction and that there

---

1. See Defendant's Memorandum of Law in Support of Motion to Dismiss Complaint at 1, *V.E.W., Ltd. v. The Vera Co.*, 2007 WL 1370469 (S.D.N.Y.).
2. *Id.*

was no valid case or controversy to uphold jurisdiction.[3] Ultimately, the case was settled outside of court. While the terms of the settlement are not known publicly, Vera Wang is selling her line of products under the "Simply Vera Vera Wang" name.

# Fashion Law Fact:

There is no law that governs the uniform sizing of garments. Although recommended industry standards and guidelines exist, they are merely suggestive.[4]

3. *Id.* at 8.
4. *Vanity Sizing*, FASHION LAW WIKI, http://fashionlawwiki.pbworks.com/w/page/11611269/Vanity%20Sizing (last visited May 22, 2013)

# Chapter Eight

# Contributory Trademark Infringement and the Fashion World

*Tiffany (NJ), Inc. v. eBay, Inc.*, 600 F.3d 93 (2d Cir. 2010).

*Louis Vuitton Malletier v. Akanoc Solutions*, 658 F.3d 936 (9th Cir. 2011).

Some things are just iconic: Jackie O's sunglasses, Madonna's bra, and of course, Tiffany's blue boxes all come to mind. Although icons can be idolized, they are also sometimes imitated—in some cases, fraudulently or in the form of counter-feit materials.

There is no question that the law protects the holders of trade-marks and copyrights against direct infringement. However, does that protection extend to contributory infringement actions? In other words, could courts hold liable a third party who does not directly participate in unlawful copyright or trademark infringe-ment, but who somehow aids, facilitates, or allows others to do so?

Take, for example, the owner of a website that allows people to trade or sell items to others. If one of the sellers lists for sale an item that the seller claims to be genuine but is in fact counterfeit and infringes on the rights of a trademark owner, can the owner of the website be liable to the owner of the mark?

That was the question the court addressed in *Tiffany (NJ), Inc. v. eBay, Inc.*[1] The court in that case declined to hold the third party—here, internet marketplace giant eBay—liable for infringement committed by its users, sellers of items in regard to fake items.

Tiffany sued eBay after discovering that some eBay users sold counterfeit Tiffany merchandise. Tiffany claimed direct infringement by eBay, claiming that eBay used the Tiffany logo to advertise on its website and in "sponsored" ad links through the websites Google and Yahoo!, sometimes advertising items that turned out to be counterfeit. Tiffany also claimed that eBay engaged in indirect, or contributory, infringement when it facilitated the sales of counterfeit items by allowing people to use eBay for those sales, along with trademark dilution and false advertising claims. A federal district court held for eBay on all counts, and Tiffany appealed.

The appellate court first discussed eBay's conduct and found that eBay took significant steps to develop antifraud measures and protect consumers and trademark holders alike.[2] In fact, the court said eBay spent as much as $20 million each year to promote trust and safety on the website.[3] Some of those steps, according to the court, included

- buyer protection programs to reimburse buyers for the cost of items that were discovered not to be genuine;
- a "Trust and Safety" department with some 4,000 employees;
- a "fraud engine" to ferret out illegal and counterfeit listings, which incorporated "Tiffany-specific filters";
- a "Verified Rights Owner" program; and

---

1. *Tiffany (NJ), Inc. v. eBay, Inc.*, 600 F.3d 93 (2d Cir. 2010).
2. *Id.* at 98.
3. *Id.* at 98.

- special warning messages when a seller attempted to list a Tiffany item.

The court noted that by late 2006, eBay had implemented additional antifraud measures, including: "delaying the ability of buyers to view listings of certain brand names, including Tiffany's, for 6 to 12 hours so as to give rights-holders such as Tiffany more time to review those listings; developing the ability to assess the number of items listed in a given listing; and restricting one-day and three-day auctions and cross-border trading for some brand-name items. . . . The district court concluded that 'eBay consistently took steps to improve its technology and develop anti-fraud measures as such measures became technologically feasible and reasonably available.'"[4]

As to the direct infringement claim, the court held that eBay committed none. "We have recognized that a defendant may lawfully use a plaintiff's trademark where doing so is necessary to describe the plaintiff's product and does not imply a false affiliation or endorsement by the plaintiff of the defendant." Here, "eBay used the [Tiffany] mark to describe accurately the genuine Tiffany goods offered for sale on its website. And none of eBay's uses of the mark suggested that Tiffany affiliated itself with eBay or endorsed the sale of its products through eBay's website."[5]

The court declined to hold eBay liable under Tiffany's contributory infringement claim as well, agreeing with district court. "For contributory trademark infringement liability to lie, a service provider must have more than a general knowledge or reason to know that its service is being used to sell counterfeit goods. . . . Some contemporary knowledge of which particular listings are

---

4. *Id.* at 100.
5. *Id.* at 103.

infringing or will infringe in the future is necessary."[6] The court noted two ways under which a service provider could be contributorily liable: by intentionally inducing a user to infringe a mark (which Tiffany did not argue) or by continuing to supply services to a user whom it knows to be engaging in infringement (which was the basis of Tiffany's claim). The court noted eBay promptly removed listings that were challenged by Tiffany, warning both sellers and buyers and canceling fees earned by eBay. It also suspended repeat offenders.

Moreover, the court rejected the argument of Tiffany, along with amici curiae from the fashion world, that making retailers police online listings for infringements will produce a burden that most mark holders cannot bear. While service providers are certainly not permitted to engage in "willful blindness,"[7] private market forces dictate that service providers minimize counterfeit goods sold on their websites to protect their reputations and enhance trust among customers and sellers alike.[8]

Some other courts, however, have treated the issue of contributory infringement on the Internet differently. As part of a footnote, the circuit court in *eBay* referred to French courts' holding that eBay violated applicable trademark laws.[9]

In *Louis Vuitton Malletier v. Akanoc Solutions*, the United States Court of Appeals for the Ninth Circuit did hold a third party Internet provider liable for counterfeiting by those who used the provider's services.[10] In that case, Louis Vuitton sued after discovering websites that sold goods that the company believed infringed its copyrights and trademarks. Rather than selling merchandise

---

6. *Id.* at 107.
7. *Id.* at 109.
8. *Id.*
9. *Id.* at ??
10. *Louis Vuitton Malletier v. Akanoc Solutions*, 658 F.3d 936 (9th Cir. 2011).

*"Don't be into trends. Don't make fashion own you, but you decide what you are, what you want to express by the way you dress and the way you live."*

**— GIANNI VERSACE**

directly, the websites listed an e-mail address for transacting the sale. The corresponding IP addresses turned out to be assigned to the defendants, Akanoc and Managed Solutions Group, which were both in the web hosting business and both managed by a third defendant, Steven Chen.

Unlike in the previous *eBay* case, the plaintiff's notices of infringement to the defendants went unanswered and unheralded by MSG, Akanoc, and Chen. At the trial level, a jury returned a verdict for Louis Vuitton against all three defendants, awarding $31,500,000 in statutory damages for willful contributory trademark infringement and another $900,000 for willful copyright infringement. After the verdict, the trial judge granted MSG's motion for judgment as a matter of law, allowing the rest of the judgment to stand and entering a permanent injunction against Akanoc and Chen.

On appeal, the Ninth Circuit court affirmed. It held that no evidence was presented at trial showing that MSG hosted the direct infringers' websites; MSG did not sell domain names or operate the servers, but merely owned and leased the hardware operated by the other two defendants.[11]

As to Akanoc and Chen, however, the appellate court affirmed the judgment, although lowering the damages to $10,500,000 for trademark infringement and $300,000 for copyright infringement and making the two defendants jointly and severally liable. "Websites are not ethereal; while they exist, virtually, in cyberspace, they would not exist at all without physical roots in servers and Internet services. . . ."[12] Appellants had control over the services and servers provided to the websites. Stated another way, [a]ppellants had direct control over the 'master switch' that kept the websites online and available."[13]

---

11. *Id.* at 942.
12. *Id.*
13. *Id* at 943.

# Chapter Nine

# Tackling the Counterfeiters

*Hard Rock Cafe Licensing Corp. v. Concession Servs., Inc.*, 955 F.2d 1143 (7th Cir. 1992).

*Burberry Ltd. v. Euro Moda*, 2009 WL 1675080 (S.D.N.Y. 2009).

A ccording to the Organisation for Economic Co-operation and Development (OECD), "Counterfeit clothing, both fashion and sportswear, is very prevalent in Europe. A common technique is to import plain clothing and attach the labels in one EU [m]ember [s]tate and then release the products for sale in another [m]ember [s]tate, benefiting from the free movement of goods across borders. . . .[1] It is a common technique to import plain clothing in one batch, produce the labels on-site or import them in another batch at another date, and then attach the labels over night close to the point of sale. This makes it much more difficult to detect the fakes while they are still in sufficiently large quantities to justify action."[2]

---

1. Report from Organisation for Economic Co-operation and Development on The Economic Impact of Counterfeiting 3 (1998) (available at http://www.oecd.org/sti/ind/2090589.pdf )
2. *Id.* at 12.

Counterfeiting is big business—in fact, the OECD reports that it is now estimated that counterfeit goods are worth more than five percent of world trade.[3] The loss to legitimate designers and manufacturers is further exacerbated by what the OECD refers to as a "lax attitude" among enforcement and a belief that counterfeiting is a "soft crime."[4] Furthermore, "[t]here is no international trade association for the fashion industry. Most luxury brand owners employ in-house anticounterfeiting officers and are members of national pan-industry counterfeiting associations."[5]

As a result of counterfeiting, industry loses billions of dollars in profit, and companies in the United States are hit hard.[6] In fact, some estimates report as much as a 16 percent loss of exports by the United States due to counterfeiting.[7]

To combat the staggering numbers, some companies have taken to the courts. In *Hard Rock Cafe Licensing Corp. v. Concession Serv.s, Inc.*, Hard Rock Cafe sued several defendants for selling counterfeit shirts that bore the company's logo.[8] Among the defendants was the seller of the shirts at flea markets, the owner of a store that sold T-shirts and other merchandise (Harry's Sweat Shop), and the owners of the flea markets in question (Concession Services Incorporated [CSI]). Most defendants settled, but Harry's and CSI went to trial.[9]

During the trial, Hard Rock explained that "recognizing counterfeit Hard Rock goods was apparently easy. . . . Any shirt not sold in a Hard Rock Cafe restaurant, was, unless second-hand,

---

3. *Id.* at 4.
4. *Id.* at 12.
5. *Id.*
6. *Id.* at 22.
7. *Id.* at 25.
8. *Hard Rock Cafe Licensing Corp. v. Concession Servs., Inc.*, 955 F.2d 1143 (7th Cir. 1992).
9. *Id.* at 1146–48.

counterfeit."[10] Harry's was found to have four purportedly counterfeit Hard Rock shirts for sale, but CSI's flea market sellers offered more than a hundred.[11]

After a bench trial, the district court found that both defendants violated the federal Lanham Act. The court entered temporary restraining orders and eventually permanent injunctions, forbidding Harry's to sell trademarked merchandise and forbidding CSI from allowing the sale of such trademarked merchandise in its locations. The court also granted treble damages against Harry's but did not grant attorneys' fees. Both defendants appealed.[12]

The appellate court vacated the trial judgment and remanded the case for further proceedings, holding that there were several factual findings that were not reached and suggesting that the trial court may have used an incorrect or insufficient standard in determining that CSI was liable. A more accurate question was whether CSI was contributorily or vicariously liable for the actions of its vendors, who brought in counterfeit merchandise. CSI argued that its relationship with the vendors was similar to that between landlord and tenant. Hard Rock agued to the contrary that CSI's role was greater (in selling tickets and overseeing admissions, for example) and that CSI should have taken precautions to protect against the sale of counterfeit products at its flea markets.[13]

"[W]e must ask whether the operator of a flea market is more like the manufacturer of a mislabeled good or more like a temporary help service supplying the purveyor of goods," the court stated.[14] "CSI may be liable for trademark violations by Parvez if it knew or had reason to know of them. But the factual findings

---

10. *Id.* at 1147.
11. *Id.* at 1148.
12. *Id.*
13. *Id.* at 1148–50.
14. *Id.* at 1148.

must support that conclusion."[15] Noting that the "willful blindness" standard applies to CSI's conduct, the court did state that CSI had no affirmative duty to seek out and prevent violations.[16]

In another case, famous high-end designer and manufacturer Burberry sued several defendants in federal district court for infringing Burberry's marks, including the well-recognized checkered pattern used famously by the company.[17]

The parties had originally settled their dispute, with the defendants acknowledging in the settlement agreement that they had purchased and sold nearly 75,000 counterfeit Burberry items, including jackets, scarves, polo shirts, and hats. As per the settlement agreement, the defendants agreed that they would refrain from causing, enabling, or assisting with any further infringements.[18]

But the honeymoon did not last long. Just a few months later, Burberry discovered more counterfeit merchandise that was sold to retailers by the defendants. Burberry sued and filed for summary judgment on the issue of liability. None of the defendants submitted an opposition to Burberry's motion.[19]

The district court granted Burberry's motion, noting that in cases where counterfeit marks were involved, it was not necessary for the plaintiff to prove the factors involved in the "likelihood of confusion" test, because counterfeit marks are inherently confusing.[20] Citing to the Lanham Act, the court defined a counterfeit mark as "a spurious mark [that] is identical with, or substantially indistinguishable from, a registered mark."[21] In this case, Burberry clearly had registered its marks, and the defendants had clearly infringed

---

15. *Id.* at 1149–50.
16. *Id.* at 1150.
17. *Burberry Ltd. v. Euro Moda*, 2009 WL 1675080 (S.D.N.Y., 2009).
18. *Id.* at 2.
19. *Id.* at 3–4.
20. *Id.* at 5.
21. *Id.* at 14, citing to 15 U.S.C. § 1127

by using counterfeit marks. "There is no distinction between the junior and senior marks. . . ."[22] Further, there is no question that Euro Moda's and Moda Oggi's use of counterfeit Burberry Marks was willfully deceptive since deceiving customers—or, in some cases, other sellers—is the whole point of creating counterfeit merchandise."[23]

## Fashion Law Fact:

A counterfeit handbag that is sold for $100 can cost as little as $1.25 to manufacture and ship from China.[24]

---

22. *Id.* at 15.
23. *Id.*
24. Anthony Ramirez, *Chinatown Journal; On Canal St., Ferreting Out the Louis Vuitton Imposters*, N.Y. Times, Jan. 29, 2006, http://query.nytimes.com/gst/fullpage.html?res=9D02E2DE1E3FF93AA15752C0A9609C8B63

# Fashion Law and Business, Trade, Litigation, and Consumer Protection

*"Fashion has two purposes: comfort and love. Beauty comes when fashion succeeds."*

**— COCO CHANEL**

# Chapter Ten

# How Much Is That Couture in the Window?:

## Fashion, Minimum Resale Prices, and Antitrust Regulations

*Leegin v. PSKS*, 127 S. Ct. 2705 (2007).

S ection 1 of the Sherman Act prohibits "[e]very contract, combination in the form of trust or otherwise, or conspiracy, in restraint of trade or commerce among the several States."[1]

In the landmark case of *Leegin v. PSKS*, the U.S. Supreme Court addressed whether vertical price restraints are per se unlawful, or whether the per se rule should be overruled and resale price agreements should be judged by the rule of reason.[2]

The case involved Leegin Creative Leather Products, Inc., which was a designer, manufacturer, and distributor of leather goods and accessories. In 1991, Leegin began to sell belts under the brand name Brighton, which was later expanded into a line of women's

---

1. 15 U.S.C. § 1 (1890)
2. *Leegin v. PSKS*, 127 S. Ct. 2705 (2007).

accessories. The plaintiff, PSKS, owned a store named Kay's Kloset, which carried the Brighton brand belts on its shelves. In 1997, Leegin instituted the Brighton Retail Pricing and Promotion Policy, by which it refused to sell its products to any retailer that discounted Brighton goods below the suggested retail prices.[3] When Leegin discovered that the plaintiff retailer had been discounting the goods in question, it elected to terminate its contract with the plaintiff's retail stores; as a result, the plaintiff lost significant business and revenue.

The plaintiff sued, and in the trial court, the jury ultimately awarded PSKS $1.2 million. The district court then trebled the damages and awarded attorneys' fees and costs for a total of $3,975,000.80.

The Court of Appeals for the Fifth Circuit affirmed, and the United States Supreme Court granted certiorari.[4] In the Supreme Court, the plaintiff retailer argued that section 1 of the Sherman Act made it per se illegal for a manufacturer and its distributor to agree on the minimum price that the distributor can charge for the manufacturer's products.

The plaintiff relied on a 1911 case, *Dr. Miles Medical Co. v. John D. Park & Sons Co.*, which decided on a per se rule.[5] The Supreme Court in this case, however, disagreed. "The rule of reason is the accepted standard for testing whether a practice restrains trade in violation of s[ection] 1," the court explained, noting that under this rule, the totality of circumstances should be weighed to decide whether a restrictive practice should be banned because it imposes unreasonable restraint on competition.[6]

---

3. *Id.* 2710–12.
4. *Id.* at 2712.
5. *Dr. Miles Medical Co. v. John D. Park & Sons Co.*, 220 U.S. 373 (1911).
6. *Leegin*, supra note 152, at 2712.

The Supreme Court noted that the per se rule should be reserved to restraints that would almost always restrain competition and decrease output, those that have "manifestly anticompetitive" effects.[7] The court relied on both legal and economic arguments, noting that minimum resale price maintenance can stimulate and increase interbrand competition (that is, competition between different brands) and make way for new entries into the market, all the while minimizing intrabrand competition (that is, competition between retailers selling the same brands).[8]

"Per se rules may decrease administrative costs, but that is only a part of the equation. . . . Those rules can be counterproductive. They can increase the total cost of the antitrust system by prohibiting precompetitive conduct the antitrust laws should encourage."[9]

# Fashion Law Fact:

The U.S. Code prohibits the importation of dog and cat fur products (with an exception carved out for personal pets who are deceased and have been preserved).[10]

---

7.  *Id.* at 2713.
8.  *Id.* at 2714–16.
9.  *Id.* at 2718.
10. 19 U.S.C. § 1308

# Chapter Eleven

# Slaving Away and Sweating for the Shop:

## Fashion and Labor Law

*Zeng Liu v. Donna Karan Int'l,* 2001 WL 8595 (S.D.N.Y. 2001).

A 2000 class-action suit was brought on behalf of Chinese immigrant workers who were employed in a garment factory against several defendants. which included the Donna Karan Company. The plaintiff class members alleged violations of the federal Fair Labor Standards Act (FLSA) and state minimum-wage statutes. They alleged that they worked 80-hour weeks but were never paid overtime and that their income amounted to less than minimum wage.[1] Although the plaintiffs were technically employed by the Chens, who owned the garment factories in question, the plaintiffs argued that Donna Karan was jointly responsible for their mistreatment.[2]

Donna Karan moved to dismiss the lawsuit, arguing that the plaintiffs failed to state a cause of action upon which relief could be granted. Specifically, the company argued that the plaintiffs'

---

1. *Zeng Liu v. Donna Karan International,* 2001 WL 8595, 1 (S.D.N.Y. 2001).
2. *Id.*

complaint failed to properly allege that Donna Karan was a joint employer of the plaintiffs under the FLSA.

The court denied the motion. It noted that the complaint alleged 60–100 percent of the clothing made in the Chens' factories was for Donna Karan, that Donna Karan directed the price and production of the garments, that it had representatives in the factory on a regular basis, and that it controlled the wages and hours of the workers through price-setting and large output demands.[3] Therefore, the court held that the plaintiffs' complaint stated enough to survive an initial motion to dismiss.[4]

In discussing the case, the court applied the standards set forth in a previous case, *Lopez v. Silverman*.[5] That similar case addressed the question of whether Renaissance Sportswear, Inc., a garment manufacturer, would be held liable as a joint employer of the plaintiff employees who had worked in a sewing and pressing operation. As in *Donna Karan*, the plaintiffs in the *Lopez* case claimed that they were not properly compensated for their overtime hours. The court there looked at the totality of circumstances to hold that the defendant, which had frequent quality control inspections and dictated deadlines for producing garments, was indeed a joint employer of the plaintiff garment workers.[6]

Although the *Donna Karan* suit was ultimately settled, the decision is an important one in the field of fashion law. As the Fashion Law Wiki, which was organized by the Fashion Law Institute, explains:

"The *Donna Karan* litigation is important precedent because Donna Karan is a well-known designer that manufactures its clothing in the same way as many other designers. Therefore, it serves

---

3. *Id.* at 3.
4. *Id.* at 4.
5. *Lopez v. Silverman*, 14 F. Supp. 2d 405 (S.D.N.Y. 1998).
6. *Id.* at 20.

as a warning to these designers that they may be held liable under joint employer doctrine for any labor law violations occurring at their garment factories despite the workers' immigration status. Although the fashion industry may find the court's decisions somewhat shocking, the outcomes are not controversial from a precedential legal perspective.

In light of this decision and for other economic reasons as well, many designers have chosen to move their garment manufacturing overseas where labor laws are less stringent. Although distasteful to workers' rights advocates, there is often little that can be done to impose sanctions on designers who take advantage of these avenues for cheap labor."[7]

# Fashion Law Fact:

So-called blood diamonds or conflict diamonds, which are diamonds sold to fund armed conflict, are worth billions of dollars and have been used to fund wars that have cost an estimated 3.7 million lives.[8] In 2003, a government-run initiative called the Kimberley Process Certification Scheme was introduced, requiring participants to certify that their shipments of rough diamonds are conflict-free.[9]

7.  *Donna Karen: Fashion and Labor Law,* FASHION LAW WIKI, http://fashionlaw-wiki.pbworks.com/w/page/11611180/Donna%20Karan%3A%20Fashion%20and%20Labor%20Law (last visited May 22, 2013)

8.  Amnesty International, *Conflict Diamonds: Did Somebody Die for That Diamond?*, AMNESTYUSA.ORG, http://www.amnestyusa.org/our-work/issues/business-and-human-rights/oil-gas-and-mining-industries/conflict-diamonds (last visited May 22, 2013

9.  *Id.*

# Chapter Twelve

# Express Yourself:
## Fashion as Expression under the First Amendment

*Tinker v. Des Moines Sch. Dist.*, 393 U.S. 503 (1969).

*H. v. Easton Area Sch. Dist.*, No. 10–6283 (E.D. Pa. 2011).

Whether it's garments or accessories, fashion often serves as a manner of self-expression. Of course, manners of expression are protected by the First Amendment to the United States Constitution. What if, however, fashion is used as self-expression by students in public school? Are they entitled to the same level of protection as other citizens?

That question was answered in the landmark case of *Tinker v. Des Moines School District*, which involved a group of students in Des Moines, Iowa, who, in December 1965, sought to publicize their opinions regarding the Vietnam War and their objections to the conflict by wearing black armbands during the holiday season. When the principals of Des Moines schools became aware of the students' plans, they adopted a policy that any student wearing an armband to school would be asked to remove it; upon refusal, students would be suspended until they returned without an armband.[1]

---

1. *Tinker v. Des Moines Sch.Dist.*, 393 U.S. 503 (1969).

The plaintiff students wore their armbands to school and were suspended. They sued the school district, seeking an injunction that would restrain the schools from disciplining the students, along with damages. Ultimately, the case made its way up to the United States Supreme Court in a 1969 decision.

The Supreme Court sided with the students, recognizing their First Amendment right to pure speech, and holding that absent clear substantial disruption to the learning process, the students' free expression rights could not be limited.[2]

"The school officials banned and sought to punish petitioners for a silent, passive expression of opinion, unaccompanied by any disorder or disturbance on the part of petitioners. There is here no evidence whatever of petitioners' interference, actual or nascent, with the schools' work or of collision with the rights of other students to be secure and to be let alone. Accordingly, this case does not concern speech or action that intrudes upon the work of the schools or the rights of other students. . . .[3] [I]n our system, undifferentiated fear or apprehension of disturbance is not enough to overcome the right to freedom of expression. Any departure from absolute regimentation may cause trouble. Any variation from the majority's opinion may inspire fear. Any word spoken, in class, in the lunchroom, or on the campus, that deviates from the views of another person may start an argument or cause a disturbance. But our Constitution says we must take this risk . . . and our history says that it is this sort of hazardous freedom— this kind of openness—that is the basis of our national strength and of the independence and vigor of Americans who grow up and live in this relatively permissive, often disputatious, society."[4]

---

2. *Id.* at 508–510.
3. *Id.* at 508.
4. *Id.* at 508–509.

*"Fashion that does not reach the streets is not fashion."*

— COCO CHANEL

As with any landmark case, the *Tinker* standard has been subjected to a number of exceptions and limitations over the years. One of those limitations arose in the case of *Bethel School District v. Fraser*, which carved out an exception to *Tinker* in cases of student speech that is lewd or vulgar.[5] The *Fraser* case had involved a student who delivered a speech before a school assembly to nominate a peer for student office; the speech was centered on an elaborate and explicit sexual metaphor. In that case, the Supreme Court held, the school could prohibit lewd, vulgar, or indecent speech, even in the absence of a substantial disruption.[6]

In recent times, that particular exception to *Tinker* has once again been addressed in cases dealing with garments and accessories worn by students. A prime example is a Pennsylvania case involving a middle school's ban on breast cancer awareness bracelets that bear the slogan "I <3 Boobies! (Keep a Breast)" and similar statements.[7] Like in *Tinker*, the students in that case sought an injunction against their middle school when they were suspended

---

5. *Bethel Sch. Dist. v. Fraser*, 478 U.S. 675 (1986).
6. *Id.* at 684–686.
7. *H. v. Easton Area Sch. Dist.*, No. 10-6283 (E.D. Pa. 2011).

and prohibited from attending a school dance, after they refused to obey the school's prohibition on wearing the bracelets in question.

The school district argued that, under *Fraser*, the bracelets were obscene and offensive and the school had the power to curb the students' free expression rights as a result.

The district court disagreed:

"[T]hese bracelets cannot reasonably be considered lewd or vulgar under the standard of *Fraser*. The bracelets are intended to be and they can reasonably be viewed as speech designed to raise awareness of breast cancer and to reduce stigma associated with openly discussing breast health. Nor has the school district presented evidence of a well-founded expectation of material and substantial disruption from wearing these bracelets under *Tinker*. The [c]ourt will therefore grant the plaintiffs' motion for preliminary injunction."[8]

The appeals court will be hearing the case en banc, on appeal by the school district.

# Fashion Law Fact:

"U.S. cities began to adopt laws prohibiting cross-dressing in the mid-1800s, although the purpose of the laws and the groups targeted shifted over the years. St. Louis, for example, adopted Ordinance No. 5421 in 1864, which stated: 'Whoever shall, in this city, appear in any public place in a state of nudity,

---

8. *Id.* at 2.

or in a dress not belonging to his or her sex, or in an indecent or lewd dress . . . shall be deemed guilty of a misdemeanor.' By the turn of the century, dozens of cities had similar laws that targeted cross-dressing."[9]

---

9.   *Cross-Dressing and the Law*, FASHION LAW WIKI, http://fashionlawwiki.pbworks. com/w/page/11611171/Cross-Dressing%20and%20the%20Law (last visited May 22, 2013)

# Chapter Thirteen

# Fashion and Beauty as Religious Apparel

*Goldman v. Weinberger*, 475 U.S. 503 (1986).

*Xodus v. Wackenhut Corp.*, No. 09–3082 (7th Cir. 2010).

F ashion and beauty often serve as a means of self-expression. In some cases, apparel, accessories, and even hairstyles can serve as expression of one's religious beliefs.

The case of *Goldman v. Weinberger* involved an Orthodox Jew and ordained rabbi who had joined the air force, serving as a clinical psychologist at the mental health clinic at March Air Force Base in Riverside, California. As part of his religious apparel, the plaintiff wore his yarmulke on the base and wore his service cap over the yarmulke when he went outdoors. The air force had a regulation in place that prohibited the wearing of headgear indoors except by armed security police in the performance of their duties. In 1981, after the plaintiff testified as a witness in a court-martial proceeding while wearing his yarmulke but not his service cap, a complaint was lodged against him, claiming that the plaintiff's practice violated the pertinent air force regulation. The plaintiff was prohibited from wearing his yarmulke indoors.[1]

He sued the secretary of defense and others, claiming that the prohibition against his wearing his yarmulke infringed upon his First Amendment freedom to exercise his religious beliefs. The district court initially enjoined enforcement of the regulation, but the appellate court reversed that decision, claiming that the air force's interest in having standardized uniforms rendered the strict enforcement of this regulation permissible.[2]

The United States Supreme Court agreed with the appeals court and affirmed its judgment. The court noted that the military was a specialized society, by necessity, which was separate from civilian society. It held: "The considered professional judgment of the [a]ir [f]orce is that the traditional outfitting of personnel in standardized uniforms encourages the subordination of personal preferences and identities in favor of the overall group mission. Uniforms encourage a sense of hierarchical unity by tending to eliminate outward individual distinctions except for those of rank."[3]

While First Amendment protections are clearly exceptionally important, their enforcement by the military takes on a different standard. "Our review of military regulations challenged on First Amendment grounds is far more deferential than constitutional review of similar laws or regulations designed for civilian society. The military need not encourage debate or tolerate protest to the extent that such tolerance is required of the civilian state by the First Amendment; to accomplish its mission, the military must foster instinctive obedience, unity, commitment, and *esprit de corps*."[4]

---

1. *Goldman v. Weinberger*, 475 U.S. 503 (1986).
2. *Id.* at 506.
3. *Id.* at 508.
4. *Id.* at 507.

*"There is no beauty that is attractive without zest."*

— CHRISTIAN DIOR

In another case—this one involving a potential employer in the private sector—a plaintiff 's religious practice claim was based on his hairstyle: dreadlocks. *Xodus v. Wackenhut Corp.* involved a suit for religious discrimination by a plaintiff who practiced the Rastafarian faith.[5] As the court explained: "A dreadlock is a 'ropelike strand of hair formed by matting or braiding.' [citation omitted] Rastafarians believe dreadlocks symbolize a bond with God, citing this passage in the Bible: '[N]o razor shall come upon his head; ☒ and he shall let the locks of hair of his head grow long.' [citation omitted]"[6]

The plaintiff applied for a position at the defendant security firm and was told during his interview that he would need to cut his dreadlocks to comply with the company's grooming policies. When Xodus refused, stating that cutting his hair was against his beliefs, he was not given the security position. Xodus sued the company, claiming that it engaged in religious discrimination when it refused to hire him based on his dreadlocks.

---

5. *Xodus v. Wackenhut Corp.*, No. 09-3082 (7th Cir. 2010).
6. *Id.*

The district court denied the defendant's motion for summary judgment on the issue of liability and held that a genuine issue of material fact existed as to whether the plaintiff had informed the defendant of his religious beliefs. "During his two-day bench trial, Xodus had to prove that he had a religious practice that conflicted with one of Wackenhut's employment requirements, that he brought his religious practice to the company's attention, and that [his religious practice] was the basis for Wackenhut's refusal to hire."[7] During the trial, differing statements emerged about whether the defendant was apprised of the plaintiff's beliefs; ultimately, the judge found McCuller more credible than Xodus and found McCuller's testimony internally consistent and corroborated.

The appeals court affirmed the lower court's decision, holding that the plaintiff's dreadlocks and his use of the word *beliefs* were not sufficient to notify the defendant of the religious nature of his hairstyle. The court concluded that "unlike race or sex, a person's religion is not always readily apparent."[8]

# Fashion Law Fact:

In 2011, several bar associations began launching dedicated fashion law groups and committees.[9]

---

7. *Id.*

8. *Id.*

9. See New York County Lawyers' Association, *New York County Lawyers Association Launches Fashion Law Subcommittee* , PITCHENGINE.COM, http://www.pitchengine.com/nycla/new-york-county-lawyers-association-launches-fashion-law-subcommittee (last visited May 22, 2013)

# Chapter Fourteen

# Fashion Law and Consumer Protection:

## FTC Regulations Regarding Garment Labels

ecause fashion is something that becomes intimately con-
nected to the human body, it is no surprise that several
regulatory protections exist in the realm of fashion law. The
Federal Trade Commission (FTC) has the following rules in place.
First, the rules establish who is covered by them:

If you manufacture, import, sell, offer to sell, distribute, or
advertise products covered by the Textile and Wool Acts, you
must comply with the labeling requirements.

You are exempt if you are:

- [a] common carrier or contract carrier shipping or delivering
  textile products in the ordinary course of business;
- [a] processor or finisher working under contract to a manufacturer (unless you change the fiber content contrary to the
  terms of the contract);

- [a] manufacturer or seller of textile products for export only; or
- [a]n advertising agency or publisher disseminating ads or promotional material about textile products.[1]

Next, the rules define what types of products are covered by these regulations:

In general, most clothing and textile products commonly used in a household are covered by the labeling requirements. Such items include:

- Clothing (except for hats and shoes — see p. 3)
- Handkerchiefs
- Scarves
- Bedding—sheets, covers, blankets, comforters, pillows, pillowcases, quilts, bedspreads, and pads (but not outer coverings for mattresses or box springs)
- Curtains and casements
- Draperies
- Tablecloths, napkins, and doilies
- Floor coverings—rugs, carpets, mats
- Towels, washcloths, and dishcloths
- Ironing board covers and pads[2]
- Umbrellas and parasols
- Bats or batting

---

1.  Bureau of Consumer Protection, *Threading Your Way Through the Labeling Requirements Under the Textile and Wool Acts*, BUSINESS.FTC.GOV, http://business. ftc.gov/documents/bus21-threading-your-way-through-labeling-requirements-under-textile-and-wool-acts (last visited May 22, 2013)

2.  Id.

- Flags—with heading or more than 216 sq. inches in size
- Cushions
- All fibers, yarns and fabrics (except packaging ribbons)
- Furniture slip covers and other furniture covers
- Afghans and throws
- Sleeping bags
- Antimacassars and tidies (doilies)
- Hammocks
- Dresser and other furniture scarves

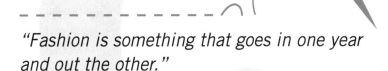

*"Fashion is something that goes in one year and out the other."*

— UNKNOWN

Next, the FTC has in place strict regulations regarding garment labeling. They are reprinted below:

## § 423.6   Textile wearing apparel.

This section applies to textile wearing apparel.

a. Manufacturers and importers must attach care labels so that they can be seen or easily found when the product is offered for sale to consumers. If the product is packaged, displayed, or folded so that customers cannot see or easily find the label, the care information must also appear on the outside of the package or on a hang tag fastened to the product.

b. Care labels must state what regular care is needed for the ordinary use of the product. In general, labels for textile wearing apparel must have either a washing instruction or a dry-cleaning instruction. If a washing instruction is included, it must comply with the requirements set forth in paragraph (b)(1) of this section. If a dry-cleaning instruction is included, it must comply with the requirements set forth in paragraph (b)(2) of this section. If either washing or dry-cleaning can be used on the product, the label need have only one of these instructions. If the product cannot be cleaned by any available cleaning method without being harmed, the label must so state. [For example, if a product would be harmed both by washing and by dry-cleaning, the label might say "Do not wash—do not dry-clean," or "Cannot be successfully cleaned."] The instructions for washing and dry-cleaning are as follows:

1. Washing, drying, ironing, bleaching and warning instructions must follow these requirements:

   i. *Washing.* The label must state whether the product should be washed by hand or machine. The label must also state a water temperature—in terms such as *cold, warm,* or *hot* —that may be used. However, if the regular use of hot water up to 145 degrees F (63 degrees C) will not harm the product, the label need not mention any water temperature. [For example, *Machine wash* means hot, warm or cold water can be used.]

   ii. *Drying.* The label must state whether the product should be dried by machine or by some other method. If machine drying is called for, the label must also state a drying temperature that may be used. However, if the regular use of a high temperature will not harm the product, the label need not mention any drying temperature. [For example, *Tumble dry* means that a high, medium, or low temperature setting can be used.]

iii. *Ironing.* Ironing must be mentioned on a label only if it will be needed on a regular basis to preserve the appearance of the product, or if it is required under paragraph (b)(1)(v) of this section, *Warnings.* If ironing is mentioned, the label must also state an ironing temperature that may be used. However, if the regular use of a hot iron will not harm the product, the label need not mention any ironing temperature.

iv. *Bleaching.*

A. If all commercially available bleaches can safely be used on a regular basis, the label need not mention bleaching.

B. If all commercially available bleaches would harm the product when used on a regular basis, the label must say "No bleach" or "Do not bleach."

C. If regular use of chlorine bleach would harm the product, but regular use of a nonchlorine bleach would not, the label must say "Only nonchlorine bleach, when needed."

v. Warnings.

A. If there is any part of the prescribed washing procedure which consumers can reasonably be expected to use that would harm the product or others being washed with it in one or more washings, the label must contain a warning to this effect. The warning must use words "Do not,"

"No," "Only," or some other clear wording. [For example, if a shirt is not colorfast, its label should state "Wash with like colors" or "Wash separately." If a pair of pants will be harmed by ironing, its label should state "Do not iron."]

B. Warnings are not necessary for any procedure that is an alternative to the procedure prescribed on the label. [For example, if an instruction states "Dry flat," it is not necessary to give the warning "Do not tumble dry."]

2. Dry-cleaning

   i. *General.* If a dry-cleaning instruction is included on the label, it must also state at least one type of solvent that may be used. However, if all commercially available types of solvent can be used, the label need not mention any types of solvent. The terms "Dry-Cleanable" or "Commercially Dry-Clean" may not be used in an instruction. [For example, if dry-cleaning in perchlorethylene would harm a coat, the label might say "Professionally dry-clean: fluorocarbon or petroleum."]

   ii. *Warnings.*

   A. If there is any part of the dry-cleaning procedure which consumers or drycleaners can reasonably be expected to use that would harm the product or others being cleaned with it, the label must contain a warning to this effect. The warning must use the words "Do not," "No," "Only," or some other clear wording. [For example, the dry-cleaning process normally includes moisture addition to solvent up to 75% relative humidity, hot tumble drying up to 160 degrees F and restoration by steam press or steam-air finish. If a product can be dry-cleaned in all solvents but steam should not be used, its label should state "Professionally dry-clean. No steam."]

B. Warnings are not necessary to any procedure which is an alternative to the procedure prescribed on the label. [For example, if an instruction states "Professionally dry-clean, fluorocarbon," it is not necessary to give the warning "Do not use perchlorethylene."]

C. A manufacturer or importer must establish a reasonable basis for care information by processing prior to sale:

1. Reliable evidence that the product was not harmed when cleaned reasonably often according to the instructions on the label, including instructions when silence has a meaning. [For example, if a shirt is labeled "Machine wash. Tumble dry. Cool iron.," the manufacturer or importer must have reliable proof that the shirt is not harmed when cleaned by machine washing (in hot water), with any type of bleach, tumble dried (at a high setting), and ironed with a cool iron]; or

2. Reliable evidence that the product or a fair sample of the product was harmed when cleaned by methods warned against on the label. However, the manufacturer or importer need not have proof of harm when silence does not constitute a warning. [For example, if a shirt is labeled "Machine wash warm. Tumble dry medium," the manufacturer need not have

proof that the shirt would be harmed if washed in hot water or dried on high setting]; or

3. Reliable evidence, like that described in paragraph (c)(1) or (2) of this section, for each component part of the product in conjunction with reliable evidence for the garment as a whole; or

4. Reliable evidence that the product or a fair sample of the product was successfully tested. The tests may simulate the care suggested or warned against on the label; or

5. Reliable evidence of current technical literature, past experience, or the industry expertise supporting the care information on the label; or

6. Other reliable evidence.[3]

In a press release dated January 3, 2013, the FTC noted that several large companies, including Amazon.com, Macy's, and Sears, "have agreed to pay penalties totaling $1.26 million to settle [FTC] charges that they violated the Textile Products Identification Act (Textile Act) and the FTC's Textile Rules by labeling and advertising products sold in stores and online as made of bamboo, while they actually were made of rayon. While so-called bamboo textiles often are promoted as environmentally friendly, the process for manufacturing rayon—even when it is made from bamboo—is far from a 'green' one."[4]

And finally, the FTC also has in place regulations regarding countries of origin of garments and fashion:

---

3. 16 C.F.R. pt. 432 (2000)

4. See *Four National Retailers Agree to Pay Penalties Totaling $1.26 Million for Allegedly Falsely Labeling Textiles as Made of Bamboo, While They Actually Were Rayon*, FTC.GOV, http://ftc.gov/opa/2013/01/bamboo.shtm (last visited May 22, 2013)

Products covered by the Textile and Wool Acts must be labeled to show the country of origin.

- Imported products must identify the country where they were processed or manufactured.
- Products made entirely in the U.S. of materials also made in the U.S. must be labeled "Made in U.S.A." or with an equivalent phrase.
- Products made in the U.S. of imported materials must be labeled to show the processing or manufacturing that takes place in the United States, as well as the imported component.
- Products manufactured in part in the U.S. and in part abroad must identify both aspects.

**Note on FTC Rules and Customs Regulations:** U.S. Customs and Border Protection has country of origin labeling requirements separate from those under the Textile and Wool Acts and Rules. For example, FTC rules do not require labeling until a textile product is in its finished state for sale to the consumer. Textile products imported in an intermediate stage may, in lieu of being labeled, be accompanied by an invoice with the required information (see p.2). Customs, however, may require that an unfinished product be marked with the country of origin. Manufacturers and importers must comply with both FTC and Customs requirements.

**Imported products made entirely abroad:** A textile product made entirely abroad must be labeled with the name of the country where it was processed or manufactured. Importers and other marketers should check Customs regulations to determine the appropriate country of origin for products made entirely abroad.

**Unqualified "Made in U.S.A." labels:** A label may say "Made in U.S.A." only if the product is made completely in the U.S. of materials that were made in the U.S. If a U.S. manufacturer uses imported greige goods that are dyed, printed, and finished in the U.S., for example, they may not be labeled "Made in U.S.A." without qualification.

**Note:** The origin of parts of the product exempt from content disclosure (such as zippers, buttons, etc.) does not have to be considered in determining the product's country of origin.

**Products made in the U.S.A. with imported materials:** The label must indicate that the product contains imported materials. The label may identify the country of origin of the imported materials, but it doesn't have to. It can say simply: "Made in U.S.A. of imported fabric" or "Knitted in U.S.A. of imported yarn." This disclosure must appear as a single statement, without separating the "Made in U.S.A." and "imported" references.

Manufacturers should be aware that for certain products— including sheets, towels, comforters, handkerchiefs, scarves, napkins, and other "flat" goods—Customs requires identification of the country where the fabric was made. To comply with Customs and FTC requirements for this group of products, the label must identify both the U.S. and the country of origin of the fabric. For example: "Made in U.S.A. of fabric made in China" or "Fabric made in China, cut and sewn in U.S.A."

**Identification of processing or manufacturing that takes place in the U.S. and abroad**

If processing or manufacturing takes place in the U.S. and another country, the label must identify both aspects of production. For example:

> Made in
> Sri Lanka,
> finished in
> U.S.A.

> Comforter
> filled,
> sewn and
> finished in
> U.S.A. with
> shell made
> in Malaysia

> Assembled
> in U.S.A.
> of imported
> components

**Note:** There are special requirements for the placement of country of origin information.

...

### Country names

The name of the country of origin must appear in English. Abbreviations (such as, U.S.A. or Gt. Britain) and other spellings close to the English version (Italie for Italy, or Brasil for Brazil) can be used if they clearly and unmistakably identify the country. Adjective forms of country names also can be used; for example,

"Chinese Silk." But the adjective form of a country name should not be used deceptively to refer to a kind or type of product, for example, "Spanish lace," when the lace is Spanish in style, but not made in Spain. Use of the abbreviations "CAN" and "MEX," for "Canada" and "Mexico," are acceptable under FTC rules, but may not be under Customs requirements.

# Fashion Law Fact:

The phrases "made in" or "product of" don't have to be used with the name of the country of origin, unless needed to avoid confusion or deception. A symbol, like a flag, could be placed next to the name of a country to indicate that the item is a product of that country. If more than one country is named on the label, phrases or words describing the specific processing in each country are usually necessary to convey the required information to the consumer."[5]

In 2011, the U.S. apparel market reportedly had total sales of $199 billion.[6]

---

5. Bureau of Consumer Protection, *Threading Your Way Through the Labeling Requirements Under the Textile and Wool Acts*, BUSINESS.FTC.GOV, http://business. ftc.gov/documents/bus21-threading-your-way-through-labeling-requirements-under-textile-and-wool-acts (last visited May 22, 2013)

6. Press Release, NPD Group, Results Show Marked Improvement Over 2010 (Mar. 29, 2012) (available at https://www.npd.com/wps/portal/npd/us/news/press-releases/pr_120329/)

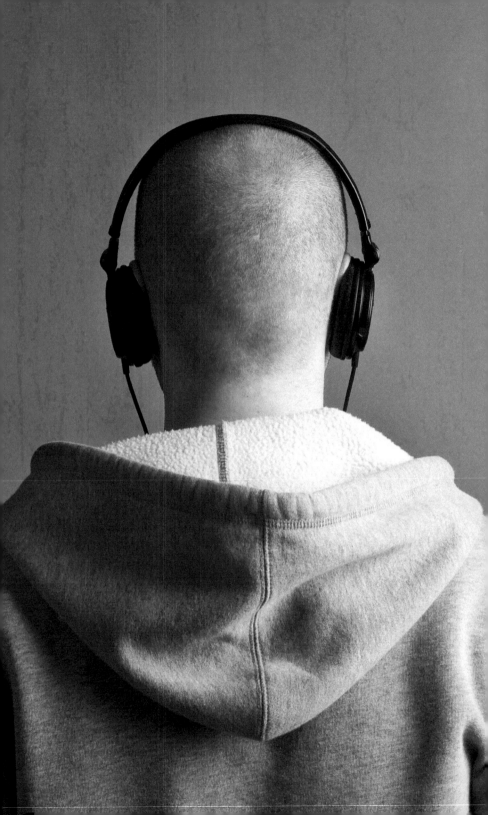

# Chapter Fifteen

# What's the Dress Code Here?:

## Laws Regarding Dress Codes

ssues with dress codes pop up in various areas and contexts from education to employment law.

In general, employers can have a dress code in place, but there are certain rules and regulations which the dress codes must follow. According to the Equal Employment Opportunity Commission website:

> In general, an employer may establish a dress code which applies to all employees or employees within certain job categories. However, there are a few possible exceptions.
>
> While an employer may require all workers to follow a uniform dress code even if the dress code conflicts with some workers' ethnic beliefs or practices, a dress code must not treat some employees less favorably because of their national origin. For example, a dress code that prohibits certain kinds of ethnic dress, such as traditional African or East Indian attire, but otherwise permits casual dress would treat some employees less favorably because of their national origin.

Moreover, if the dress code conflicts with an employee's religious practices and the employee requests an accommodation, the employer must modify the dress code or permit an exception to the dress code unless doing so would result in undue hardship.

Similarly, if an employee requests an accommodation to the dress code because of his disability, the employer must modify the dress code or permit an exception to the dress code, unless doing so would result in undue hardship.[1]

In one New York case, which took place in federal district court, an employee of a hospital sued her employer, claiming discriminatory enforcement of the hospital's dress code and retaliation against the plaintiff for bringing union grievances regarding racial discrimination. The plaintiff worked as a unit clerk in the cardiothoracic surgical intensive care unit. The defendant hospital had a dress code that expressly provided that employees' style must "be conservative and in keeping with the professional image in nursing." On one day in question, the plaintiff came to work in "a red, three-quarter-length, cowl-necked dress and red boots made of lycra fabric [that] went over her knees," over which she wore the hospital's regulation blue smock. The plaintiff also wore her hair in what she described as an "Afro hairstyle." According to the plaintiff, she was approached by a doctor and asked to look in a mirror and see what appeared, and allegedly the same doctor told the plaintiff that she "belong[ed] in a zoo" and looked like "she was going to the disco." During a formal meeting, the plaintiff was advised that she violated the hospital's dress code. She filed a grievance, which was unsuccessful.[2]

---

1. *Prohibited Employment Policies/Practices*, EEOC.GOV, http://www.eeoc.gov/laws/practices/index.cfm (last visited May 22, 2013)

2. *Ali v. Mount Sinai Hospital*, 1996 WL 325585 (S.D.N.Y. 1996).

*"The difference between style and fashion is quality."*

— **GIORGIO ARMANI**

In this case, the plaintiff claimed that the hospital retaliated against her with grievances (such as by accusing her of being rude to other staff or falsely accusing her of mislabeling blood). She also claimed that this caused her to suffer serious depression.

The district court granted the defendant's summary judgment motion on all counts. Regarding the dress code issues, the court held that the plaintiff did not sufficiently show discriminatory enforcement. "To establish a prima facie case of individualized disparate treatment from an alleged discriminatory enforcement of the dress code, plaintiff must show that she is a member of a protected class and that, at the time of the alleged discriminatory treatment, she was satisfactorily performing the duties of her position. This she has done. However, her prima facie showing must also include a showing that Mount Sinai Hospital had a dress code and that it was applied to her under circumstances giving rise to an inference of discrimination. . . .[3] [the p]laintiff offers no evidence that the dress code was not enforced against other [h]ospital employees as it was against her."[4]

---

3. *Id.* at 6.
4. *Id.* at 7.

In a more recent case, an employee of Disney filed suit against her employer, claiming religious discrimination after she claimed Disney refused to let her wear her hijab, a religious headscarf, while she worked at one of the cafes in a Disneyland hotel. The American Civil Liberties Union filed suit on the employee's behalf.[5]

Some employers get into hot water when they require their employees to purchase certain garments and wear them on the job, without compensating the employees properly. In 2009, retailer Abercrombie & Fitch (A & F) settled a suit with California labor regulators, paying out $2.2 million. The retailer allegedly forced its employees to buy and wear its clothes while on the job. Under the settlement, A & F denied any wrongdoing but agreed not to force workers to buy its clothing and to reimburse California employees for A & F-brand clothes they purchased, with reimbursement amounts ranging from $200 to $490.[6]

But work is not the only place where laws about how one can dress are popping up. In fact, some cities and states are attempting to regulate what people can wear in public. Of course, indecency laws (such as those that prohibit nude sun-bathing) have long played a big part in regulating how people can (and cannot) dress in public. But one recently attacked specific culprit? Saggy, baggy pants! Just consider the following collection of laws, according to an article in the Daily Mail:

- Florida passed a state law in 2011/12 banning the wearing of saggy pants on a three-strike policy that would lead to suspension.

---

5. Eugene W. Fields, Ex-*Disney Employee Files Discrimination Lawsuit*, ORANGE CNTY REGISTER, Aug. 13, 2012, http://www.ocregister.com/articles/disney-368457-boudlal-work.html.

6. *Employees Win Dress Code Lawsuit*, CBSNEWS.COM, Feb. 11, 2009, http://www.cbsnews.com/2100-201_162-560245.html.

- In June 2011 in Forth Worth, Texas, the local transportation authority prohibited the wearing of sagging pants on buses— on the first day of its implementation fifty people were removed from the bus.
- On December 8, 2010, the city of Opa-Locka, Florida, voted to introduce a $250 fine and ten hours of community service for people wearing saggy pants.
- On November 23, 2010, Albany, Georgia, banned the wearing of pants more than three inches below the top of the hips with a $25 penalty.
- In March 2008, the town of Hahira, Georgia, passed an indecent exposure ordinance, which prohibited wearing trousers in such a way as to show underwear.
- In June 2007, the Town Council of Delcambre, Louisiana, also passed a similar law, which banned wearing pants or slacks to show underwear.[7]

And of course, schools see their fair share of disputes over dress codes imposed on students. In 2008, a free speech lawsuit brought by the ACLU against the Napa Valley Unified School District was settled. The lawsuit was brought because of an apparently overly strict dress code at a middle school that banned various fabrics, dress, and colors—including, reportedly, Winnie the Pooh socks and jeans![8]

---

7. James Nye, *Florida City Bans Saggy Pants . . . and Is Accused of Racial Profiling for Doing It*, DAILY MAIL, Oct. 24, 2012, http://www.dailymail.co.uk/news/article-2222610/Florida-city-bans-saggy-pants--accused-racial-profiling-doing-it.html?ito=feeds-newsxml.

8. *School Dress Lawsuit Settled*, LEGALINFO.COM (Jan. 30, 2008, 3:00 PM), http://www.legalinfo.com/legal-news/school-dress-code-lawsuit-settled.html.

# Fashion Law Fact:

In December 2009, the National Intellectual Property Rights Coordination Center worked in coordination with U.S. Immigration and Customs Enforcement to coordinate Holiday Hoax, a multistate and multiagency holiday surge operation that targeted counterfeit goods in transit, at transportation hubs, and at sales retail points. The operation yielded 15 arrests and 708,250 counterfeit goods seized, worth more than $26 million.[9]

9. Fact Sheet from National IPR Coordination Center on Operation Holiday Hoax (on file with author)

# Beauty and the Law

*"The beauty of a woman is not in the clothes she wears, the figure that she carries, or the way she combs her hair. The beauty of a woman is seen in her eyes, because that is the doorway to her heart, the place where love resides. True beauty in a woman is reflected in her soul. It's the caring that she lovingly gives, the passion that she shows, and the beauty of a woman only grows with passing years."*

**— AUDREY HEPBURN**

# Chapter Sixteen

# Does it Pass the Smell Test?:

## Versions of Perfumes, Beauty Products, and Hair Care, and Intellectual Property Protections

*L'Oreal SA v. Bellure NV,* 2007 WL 2817991.

*Mixed Chicks, LLC v. Sally Beauty Supply.*

F ashion trademark infringement cases may be manifold, but the issue also arises in the world of beauty products.

In one case, famous maker L'Oreal sued Bellure NA, a beauty-product manufacturer, in European courts. L'Oreal manufactured perfumes including Tresor, Anais Anais, and Miracle, among others. The defendants manufactured and sold smell-alike perfumes, which were not only intended to smell like the perfumes made by L'Oreal but also resembled the plaintiff's perfumes in their packaging, even including comparison tables pitting the smell-alike perfume against the perfume originally manufactured by the plaintiff.[1] Of course, the products had different price points and different customer bases, and therefore, the defendants claimed, there was no infringement.

A European district court ruled that Bellure's conduct amounted to trademark and copyright infringement. On appeal, the court referred a number of questions to the European Court of Justice (ECJ). Most importantly, the court asked, did the use of comparison tables in fact amount to trademark infringement? The appellate court stated, "neither the image nor the essential function of the trade marks for the originals was adversely affected by the lists. Nobody was deceived and nobody thought any less of [L'Oreal's] brands."[2] As a result, the issue was whether the lists were in accordance with honest industry and commercial practices, or whether they amounted to "unfair advantage" within the meaning of pertinent trademark laws which was a question properly submitted to the ECJ.

The court also noted that the sales of smell-alike perfumes themselves did not amount to deception simply because L'Oreal's perfumes were well-known and another company sought to emulate them. "If what was complained of did not inherently tell a lie, it was not an instrument of deception itself."[3]

In 2012, hair product manufacturer Mixed Chicks sued Sally Beauty Supply, a known retailer of beauty products. Mixed Chicks was founded by two women with one mission: to research and manufacture novel hair care products that would cater to a multiracial female clientele.

Sally Beauty, reportedly, approached Mixed Chicks with an offer to carry its hair care products in Sally stores, but Mixed Chicks declined. In 2011, Sally Beauty came out with its own hair

---

1. *L'Oreal SA v. Bellure NV*, 2007 WL 2817991
2. *Id.*
3. *Id.*

care products for multiracial women, which it called Mixed Silk.[4] Mixed Chicks sued for trademark and trade dress infringement.

The result? Sally Beauty agreed to pay Mixed Chicks a settlement reportedly worth over $8 million.[5]

# Fashion Law Fact:

The Food and Drug Administration defines cosmetics as substances "intended to be applied to the human body for cleansing, beautifying, promoting attractiveness, or altering the appearance without affecting the body's structure or functions."[6]

4.  Lisa Schuman, *Mixed Chicks Gets $8.5M Jury Award for Infringing Mixed-Race Hair Products*, CORPORATE COUNSEL, Dec. 5, 2012, http://www.law.com/corporatecounsel/PubArticleCC.jsp?id=1202580228393&Mixed_Chicks_Gets_85M_Jury_Award_for_Infringing_MixedRace_Hair_Products&slret urn=20130002105150

5.  *Id.*

6.  U.S. FOOD AND DRUG ADMIN., *Summary of Regulatory Requirements for Labeling of Cosmetics Marketed in the United States*, in COSMETIC LABELING MANUAL (June 18, 2009) (available at http://www.fda.gov/Cosmetics/CosmeticLabelingLabelClaims/CosmeticLabelingManual/ucm126438.htm

# Chapter Seventeen

# Delegation Problems

*Sally Beauty Co., v. Nexxus Products Co.,*
801 F. 2d 1001 (7th Cir. 1986).

I s it permissible to delegate a duty under a contract to a fully-owned subsidiary of the competitor organization, or to a direct competitor organization?

In *Sally Beauty Co.. v. Nexxus Products Co.*, the appellate court said no.

That case involved a contract between Nexxus Products Company and Best Barber & Beauty Supply Company, under which Best became the exclusive distributor of Nexxus hair care products to stylists, salons, and barbers throughout the state of Texas. Nexxus canceled the contract once Best was acquired by and merged into Sally Beauty Company, Inc., which was a wholly-owned subsidiary of Alberto-Culver Company, which was another manufacturer of hair care products and a competitor of Nexxus. (Still following all of the players? Nice job!)

Sally Beauty sued Nexxus, claiming that it breached the contract by canceling. In response, Nexxus claimed that the contract was not assignable to Sally Beauty and, in fact, not assignable at all. The district court granted Nexxus's motion for summary judgment. It ruled that the contract was one for personal services and therefore not assignable at all, regardless of to whom the assignment was made.[1]

The United States Court of Appeals for the Seventh Circuit affirmed but on slightly different grounds. The court looked to the Uniform Commercial Code, which governs transactions in goods. The court explained that the contract here was not a personal service contract but rather a contract for the sale of goods.[2] However, that did not mean the contract was freely assignable under any circumstances.[3] In this case, the court was concerned as to whether Sally Beauty—a subsidiary of a competitor—could, in fact, satisfy the requirements of the contract impartially. "Sally Beauty may be totally sincere in its belief that it can operate 'impartially' as a distributor, but who can guarantee the outcome when there is a clear choice between the demands of the parent-manufacturer, Alberto-Culver, and the competing needs of Nexxus? The risk of an unfavorable outcome is not one which the law can force Nexxus to take."[4]

Siding with Nexxus, the court held "that the duty of performance under an exclusive distributorship may not be delegated to a competitor in the market place—or the wholly-owned subsidiary of a competitor—without the obligee's consent. . . ."[5] We believe that such a rule is consonant with the policies behind section 2–210, which is concerned with preserving the bargain the obligee has struck. Nexxus should not be required to accept the 'best efforts' of Sally Beauty when those efforts are subject to the control of Alberto-Culver. It is entirely reasonable that Nexxus

---

1. *Sally Beauty Co. v. Nexxus Products Co.* 801 F. 2d 1001 (7th Cir. 1986).
2. *Id.* at 1006
3. *Id.*
4. *Id.* at 1008.
5. *Id.* at 1007.

should conclude that this performance would be a different thing than what it had bargained for."[6]

# Fashion Law Fact:

Cosmetic products do not require Food and Drug Administration approval before they go on the market, with the single exception of color additives.[7]

---

6. *Id.* at 1008.

7. *Is It Really FDA Approved?*, FDA.GOV, http://www.fda.gov/ForConsumers/ConsumerUpdates/ucm047470.htm (last visited May 22, 2013)

# Chapter Eighteen

# NO-rganic Products:
## This is Not What You Promised!

*Center for Environmental Health v. Advantage Research Labs.*

With lack of strict regulation—not to mention the lack of a unified definition for words such as *green* or *cruelty-free*—it is easy to see how a cosmetic company might get away with using such labels on its products, regardless of the actual background.

The Federal Trade Commission's website advises the following:

### General Environmental Benefit Claims
- Marketers should not make broad, unqualified general environmental benefit claims like "green" or "eco-friendly." Broad claims are difficult to substantiate, if not impossible.
- Marketers should qualify general claims with specific environmental benefits. Qualifications for any claims should be clear, prominent, and specific.
  - When a marketer qualifies a general claim with a specific benefit, consumers understand the benefit to be significant. As a result, marketers shouldn't highlight small or unimportant benefits.

- If a qualified general claim conveys that a product has an overall environmental benefit because of a special attribute, marketers should analyze the trade-offs resulting from the attribute to prove the claim[1]

The label *organic* has, in some cases, been defined through statutory and regulatory means. In California, for example, the California Organic Products Act of 2003 (COPA) requires that any beauty products that are sold, marketed, labeled, or represented as organic contain at least 70 percent organic ingredients by weight.

To fight back against companies that claim to sell organic products but fail to deliver, some plaintiffs have taken to the courts. In 2011, the nonprofit corporation Center for Environmental Health sued a slew of defendants, alleging the "illegal sale of cosmetic products" by them.[2] The plaintiff claimed that defendants sold cosmetic or personal care products that were "marketed, labeled and sold as 'organic,' but which in fact contain less than 70% organic ingredients."[3] The plaintiff claimed the defendants violated COPA and sought the court to enjoin the defendants' "false and misleading labeling."[4]

Whether a beauty product is organic was just one claim made by plaintiffs. Another claim centered on the always-controversial issue of animal testing. A 2012 class-action suit against Avon Products, Inc., Estee Lauder Companies, and Mary Kay alleged that the defendants defrauded American consumers by marketing their

---

1. Bureau of Consumer Protection, *Environmental Claims: Summary of the Green Guides*, BUSINESS.FTC.GOV, http://business.ftc.gov/documents/environmental-claims-summary-green-guides (last visited May 22, 2013),
2. Complaint for Injunctive Relief at 1, *Center for Environmental Health v. Advantage Research Laboratories, Inc.* http://www.google.com/search?q=Environ mental+Claims%3A+Summary+of+theGreen+Guides%2C&rlz=1I7ADFA_en&ie=UTF-8&oe=UTF-8&sourceid=ie7 (Ca. Super. Ct. 2011).
3. *Id.*
4. *Id.* at 2.

products as "free of animal testing," when in fact, the companies allegedly tested on animals.[5]

The court dismissed the plaintiffs' claims for fraud, holding that the plaintiffs failed to state a claim upon which relief can be granted. The court noted that while the plaintiffs generally alluded to purchasing a "multitude" of the defendants' products, they did not allege with sufficient certainty which of the products had fraudulently convinced plaintiffs to purchase them. Moreover, the court noted that while the plaintiffs brought up several examples of statements made by the defendants regarding lack of animal testing (such as statements to People for Ethical Treatment of Animals made by Mary Kay and Estee Lauder, and representations to the Coalition for Consumer Information of Cosmetics), the plaintiffs nevertheless did not identify the particular misrepresentation or omission by the defendants upon which the plaintiffs relied. As a result, the court held the elements of fraud were not met under the applicable statutory provisions.[6]

## Fashion Law Fact:

Although they are not required by law, several tests are commonly performed by exposing mice, rats, rabbits, guinea pigs, and other animals to cosmetics ingredients. This can include:

---

5.   Order and Civil Minutes—General at [need page number], *Ashley Stanwood v. The Estee Lauder Companies* (No. SACV 12-003120CJC[ANx]) (C.D. Ca. 2012); see also *Beltran v. Avon products*, (No. 2;12-cv-02502-CJC [ANx]) (C.D. Ca. 2012).
6.   *Id.*

- skin and eye irritation tests where chemicals are rubbed onto the shaved skin or dripped into the eyes of restrained rabbits without any pain relief;
- repeated force-feeding studies lasting weeks or months to look for signs of general illness or specific health hazards such as cancer or birth defects; and
- widely condemned 'lethal dose' tests, in which animals are forced to swallow large amounts of a test chemical to determine the dose that causes death.

At the end of a test the animals are killed, normally by asphyxiation, neck breaking, or decapitation. Pain relief is not provided. In the United States, a large percentage of the animals used in such testing (such as laboratory-bred rats and mice) are not counted in official statistics and receive no protection under the Animal Welfare Act.[7]

---

7. Fact Sheet from Humane Society on Cosmetic Testing (July 28, 2012) (available at http://www.humanesociety.org/issues/cosmetic_testing/qa/questions_answers.html)

# Chapter Nineteen

# Beauty Biz:
## Responsibility of the Board to Maximize Immediate Stockholder Value by Securing the Highest Price Available

*Revlon, Inc. v. MacAndrews & Forbes Holdings, Inc.*, 506 A.2d 173 (Del. 1986).

The beauty business is often big business, with corporate and securities concerns giving rise to important court decisions.

In June 1985, the chairman and CEO of Revlon, Inc., negotiated with his counterpart at Pantry Pride regarding the friendly acquisition of Revlon by the company. Pantry Pride's CEO suggested a stock price of $40–$50 per share, which Revlon's CEO dismissed a "considerably below Revlon's intrinsic value."[1] In August of the same year, Pantry Pride's board authorized the CEO to acquire Revlon, either by negotiating a share price of $42–$43

---

1. *Revlon, Inc. v. MacAndrews & Forbes Holdings, Inc.*, 506 A.2d 173, 176 (Del. 1986)

or by making a hostile tender offer[2] at $45.[3] Revlon's investment banker advised its board that the $45 per share price was grossly inadequate for the company.

Revlon's board rejected the offer, fearing that the acquisition would be financed by junk bonds and result in the corporation's dissolution. To prevent Pantry Pride's hostile tender offer, the Revlon board adopted a Note Purchase Rights Plan, which would allow its stockholders to receive note purchase rights for each share of stock at a per-share rate of $65 or more, along with interest; the rights would become effective whenever anyone acquired beneficial ownership of 20 percent or more of the company's shares.[4] The new notes would contain certain covenants, limiting Revlon's ability to incur additional debts, sell assets, or pay dividends without independent authorization of the board.[5] Pantry Pride then made some subsequent offers (one at as high as $56.25 per share) that the Revlon board rejected.[6]

In the meantime, Revlon had been negotiating with Forstmann Little & Co., a private equity firm (which was known for its takeovers and named, ultimately, as a defendant in this suit). Revlon's board unanimously agreed to a leveraged buyout by Forstmann, through which Revlon's debts would be assumed, the notes covenants would be waived, and any shareholder's rights to be bought out would be redeemed, with each stockholder getting $56 per

---

2. A hostile tender offer is one which is made during a hostile takeover of a corporation. According to the Bouvier Law Dictionary, a tender offer is "a solicitation to the shareholders of a corporation to tender their shares to the offeror for purchase." *Tender offer, in* BOUVIER LAW DICTIONARY 1073 (Stephen M. Sheppard ed., 2011).

3. *Revlon* 506 A.2d 173, 176 (Del. 1986) at 176

4. *Id.*

5. *Id.* at 177.

6. *Id.* at 177–178.

share.[7] When the merger and the waiver of the notes covenants was announced, the market value of the securities began to fall.[8]

Pantry Pride ultimately sued, asking the Delaware court to grant an injunction against Revlon from engaging in the transactions that Pantry Pride claimed were designed to thwart its efforts. The trial court granted the injunction. In an appellate decision, the Supreme Court of Delaware affirmed that judgment, holding that the board of directors owed the corporation and its stockholders fiduciary duties of loyalty and care, which were breached by the board's adoption of its "poison pill" plan and gave stockholders the right to be brought out.

"When Pantry Pride increased its offer to $50 per share, and then to $53, it became apparent to all that the break-up of the company was inevitable. . . . The Revlon board's authorization permitting management to negotiate a merger or buyout with a third party was a recognition that the company was for sale. The duty of the board had thus changed from the preservation of Revlon as a corporate entity to the maximization of the company's value at a sale for the stockholders' benefit. This significantly altered the board's responsibilities under the Unocal standards. It no longer faced threats to corporate policy and effectiveness, or to the stockholders' interests, from a grossly inadequate bid. The whole question of defensive measures became moot. The directors' role changed from defenders of the corporate bastion to auctioneers charged with getting the best price for the stockholders at a sale of the company."[9]

---

7. *Id.* at 178.
8. *Id.*
9. *Id.* at 182.

# Fashion Law Fact:

The cosmetic industry grosses over $20 billion per year. The cosmetic surgery industry, by contrast, grosses over $300 billion annually.[10]

---

10. *Id.*

# Chapter Twenty

# Beauty, Looks, and Hairstyles in the Workplace

*Rogers v. Am. Airlines, Inc.*, 527 F. Supp. 229 (S.D.N.Y 1981).

*Burchette v. Abercrombie & Fitch Co.*, 2010 WL 1948322 (S.D.N.Y. 2010).

In *Rogers v. Am. Airlines, Inc.*, an employee of an airline filed a suit for gender discrimination and violation of the Thirteenth Amendment, challenging the employer's rule that prohibited employees in certain categories (namely, those who had major customer contact) from wearing an all-braided hairstyle. The plaintiff, an African American woman, alleged that the employer's denial of her right to wear her hair in a cornrow hairstyle intruded on her rights and discriminated against her.[1]

The defendants moved to dismiss the claims, and the court granted the motion, noting that an "even-handed policy that prohibits to both sexes a style more often adopted by members of one sex does not constitute prohibited sex discrimination.... The policy is addressed to both men and women, black and white. Plaintiff's assertion that the policy has practical effect only with respect to

---

1.  *Rogers v. Am. Airlines, Inc.*, 527 F. Supp. 229 (S.D.N.Y 1981).

women is not supported by any factual allegations. Many men have hair longer than many women. Some men have hair long enough to wear in braids if they choose to do so."[2]

The court, moreover, noted that the airline did not require the plaintiff to restyle her hair, but rather permitted her to put it up in a bun while on duty and warp a hairpiece around that bun. The court also acknowledged that the plaintiff did not dispute American's reasoning for adopting the policy: to project a more conservative and professional image, which the court recognized as a bona fide business purpose.[3]

In another case, The Court of Appeals for the Eleventh Circuit upheld a grooming policy by video chain Blockbuster. In *Harper v. Blockbuster Entertainment Corp.*, four male employees sued the company, claiming that the company's grooming policy (which allowed women but not men to have long hair) discriminated against them on the basis of gender and that they were wrongfully terminated in retaliation for protesting the policy.[4]

The court relied on precedent to hold that differing hair length standards did not violate Title VII, and therefore, the plaintiffs' employment discrimination claim failed.[5]

In 2008, Burchette, a female employee who identified herself as a "multiracial woman" likewise filed suit against her employer, Abercrombie & Fitch. Burchette claimed that the company discriminated against her through the selective application and enforcement of a "'look' policy [that] regulates and classifies hair color on the basis of employee race and color of skin."[6] Under the "look" policy, Burchette claimed that while white workers were

---

2. *Id.*
3. *Id.* at 233.
4. *Harper v. Blockbuster Entertainment Corp.*, 139 F. 3d 1385 (11th Cir. 1998).
5. *Id.*
6. *Burchette v. Abercrombie & Fitch Co.*, 2010 WL 1948322 (S.D.N.Y. 2010).

allowed to dye their hair "unnatural" colors (such as bleached blonde), African American workers were not allowed to use hair colors that did not appear to be "natural" together—namely, anything but black or dark brown. Burchette claimed that, upon her dying some of her hair a lighter color, her managers told her she could not return to work until she dyed her hair to its "natural" color. Burchette sued for race discrimination, selective enforcement, and hostile work environment violations.

The federal district court granted Abercrombie & Fitch's (A & F) motion for summary judgment. The court held that the plaintiff failed to "adduce evidence that would permit a trier of fact to conclude that A & F subjected her to an adverse employment action."[7] Among some of the facts highlighted by the court was that the plaintiff did not receive a notice of termination, that she had, in fact, worked longer hours during the month in which she was counseled regarding the look policy than in the past, and that she failed to introduce evidence that other employees were treated disparately regarding their hair color.

---

7. *Id.* at 7.

# Chapter Twenty-One

# "Lookism" and the Law

*Hodgdon v. Mt. Mansfield Co.*, 624 A.2d 1122 (Vt. 1992).

*Nelson v. James H. Knight, DDS, P.C.*, No. 11-1857 (Iowa 2012).

The world is full of lookism. In fact, the term is even explained in the dictionary: "Nearly everyone knows the phenomenon that you need to hand in photos for job applications, that good-looking people are the center of attention at parties, that people are subconsciously rated as too fat, too skinny, too tall, too small, as beautiful or ugly, or that one's own body can be perceived as ugly, and therefore, one feels insecure and unhappy. It is so common that billboards, magazines and TV shows almost only show people who match the dominant beauty image that it hardly attracts attention. Beauty is a market value within the competitive, capitalist society and the positive estimation of beauty leads to the discrimination of others who deviate from this constructed, bodily norm. This form of discrimination, which is prevalent in all areas of life and still hardly regarded, is called lookism."[1]

Of course, lookism can cut both ways. Cases dealing with lookism—plaintiffs who claim they were discriminated against

---

1.  www.merriam-webster.com/dictionary/lookism

for being too attractive or not being attractive enough—have found their way into courts. Who could forget the recent case of the beautiful dental assistant who was fired for being too attractive?

In *Nelson v. James H. Knight, DDS, P.C.*, the Supreme Court of Iowa wrestled with the following question: Can a male employer fire a female employee because his wife is worried about the nature of the employer-employee relationship? The court held "the conduct does not amount to unlawful sex discrimination in violation of the Iowa Civil Rights Act."[2]

In Nelson, the plaintiff dental assistant had worked for the defendant dentist for over a decade, when her employment was terminated, admittedly by the defendant, based on the plaintiff's looks. On several occasions, the defendant had complained to the plaintiff that her clothing was too tight, revealing, and distracting, and asked her to wear a lab coat. The two had texted each other on both work and personal matters outside the office. Once, when the plaintiff made a statement regarding infrequency in her sex life, the defendant reportedly responded to her that that was like "having a Lamborghini in the garage and never driving it."[3]

When the defendant's wife found out that the plaintiff and the defendant were texting each other, she confronted her husband and demanded that he terminate the plaintiff's employment. The defendant did so, and the plaintiff sued for sex discrimination— after all, she claimed, if she had not been a woman, then there would have been no basis for an attraction to her by the defendant and therefore no basis for her termination either.

The court in the *Nelson* case did not consider the defendant's actions to be motivated by gender. The court noted that "a

---

2. *Nelson v. James H. Knight, DDS, P.C*, No. 11-1857, 2, http://www.iowacourts. gov/Supreme_Court/Recent_Opinions/20121221/11-1857.pdf (Sup. Ct. of Iowa Dec. 21, 2012).

3. *Id.* at 3.

distinction exists between (1) an isolated employment decision based on personal relations (assuming no coercion or quid pro quo), even if the relations would not have existed if the employee had been of the opposite gender, and (2) a decision based on gender itself. In the former case, the decision is driven entirely by individual feelings and emotions regarding a specific person. Such a decision is not gender-based, nor is it based on factors that might be a proxy for gender."[4]

The *Nelson* court cited a 2006 case from the Eighth Circuit that likewise dealt with a personal relationship between a small business owner and an employee who was seen by the owner's wife as a threat to her marriage. In *Tenge v. Phillips Modern Ag Co.*, the plaintiff employee had a personal relationship with her employer in which she admitted that she sometimes left notes of a sexual or intimate nature for her boss in locations where other people could see them and that she had pinched the owner's rear.[5] As in *Nelson*, the defendant's wife in *Tenge* requested her husband terminate the employee who was seen as a threat. The court held "absent claims of coercion or widespread sexual favoritism, where an employee engages in consensual sexual conduct with a supervisor and an employment decision is based on this conduct, Title VII is not implicated because any benefits of the relationship are due to the sexual conduct, rather than the gender, of the employee."[6]

The court in *Nelson* did note an important distinction between that case and *Tenge*, however. In *Nelson*, the plaintiff did not engage in any consensual sexual conduct. Still, the *Nelson* court argued, the decision to fire her was ultimately not gender-based and, therefore, did not violate Title VII.[7]

---

4. *Id.* at 11.
5. *Tenge v. Phillips Modern Ag Co.*, 446 F.3d 903 (8th Cir. 2006).
6. *Id.* at 909.
7. *Nelson, supra* note 243, at 11.

Then there is the other side of the coin. Although the preceding cases dealt with plaintiffs who were "hated on" because they were beautiful, some plaintiffs sue for the opposite: not fitting a certain look that their employer wants them to have.

In *Hodgdon v. Mt. Mansfield Co., Inc.*, a former chambermaid was fired from the defendant ski resort's employment when she refused to wear dentures. The plaintiff did not have natural teeth but did have a set of dentures; however, she did not wear them because they hurt her. After a supervisory change, the plaintiff was sent a letter in which she was instructed that the resort was concerned about upgrading the image of its employees in public and that all employees were expected to have and wear teeth.[8] The plaintiff explained to her employer that she could not wear her dentures because they did not fit and asked that she be allowed to work so that she could earn enough money to purchase a new set of dentures. The employer told plaintiff that she could not return to work without dentures.

The plaintiff filed suit, claiming that the defendant violated federal law by firing her because of a perceived handicap and her gender. She also brought claims for invasion of privacy, intentional infliction of emotional distress, and wrongful discharge, some of which were dismissed. The trial court granted the defendant's motions for trial and for summary judgment on the other claims, and found that the plaintiff did not qualify as a handicapped individual under the Federal Employment Practices Act.

The Supreme Court of Vermont ultimately sided with the plaintiff, holding that she was entitled to a jury trial on her sex-discrimination claim. "We agree that plaintiff's evidence indicated that one of the maintenance workers who had lost his teeth had

---

8. *Hodgdon v. Mt. Mansfield Co., Inc.*, 624 A. 2d 1122 (Vt. 1992).

contact with the public to the same extent as the plaintiff. . . .[9] In addition, the plaintiff presented evidence indicating that other 'grooming' standards, such as those regarding hair length, were not enforced against male employees." Though the court held that the plaintiff was not entitled to a jury trial on her handicap-discrimination claim brought under FEPA (because she only sought injunctive relief) it did overturn the lower court's determination regarding the plaintiff not qualifying as a handicapped individual. Indeed, the court held, the defendant regarded or perceived the plaintiff as a handicapped individual. "[The] defendant regards plaintiff as unfit to be seen by customers. This is not a qualification unique to the position from which she was fired, but, rather, is to regard plaintiff as substantially limited in her ability to work. . . .[10] [W]hen an employer makes an employment decision based on its belief that an employee with a visible physical impairment is not fit to work in a position involving any customer contact, then the employer has treated the impairment as substantially limiting the employee's ability to work. In such circumstances, the employee is a handicapped individual under FEPA."[11]

---

9. *Id.* at 1128.
10. *Id.* at 1132.
11. *Id.*

# Chapter Twenty-Two

# Models and the Law

I t is no secret that models are expected to look a certain way—
after all, they are "modeling" a certain look or a certain product
being sold by the specific fashion or beauty company.

A big part of looking "up to industry standards," of course, deals
with weight. Fashion and beauty models' weight is one of the most
hotly debated topics in the industry. There are several arguments
for using skinny models: their lithe figures might make a designer's
duds stand out more; skinny figures have long been the standard
of beauty; and a slim silhouette (the more unattainable, the better) is something to which ordinary women—buyers and gawkers
of fashion designs—aspire.[1]

That might be the skinny, but it's also a topic under the micro-
scope—even in the world of fashion law. Following the deaths
of models whose BMI[2] was way under the recommended figures,

---

1. *Fashion Models and Weight*, FASHION LAW WIKI, http://fashionlawwiki.pbworks.
com/w/page/11611233/Models%20and%20weight (last visited May 22, 2013).

2. BMI stands for "body mass index," which is a person's body mass divided
by the square of the person's height. The World Health Organization recommends a
minimum of 18.5 BMI, under which number a person is considered "malnourished."

several attempts at regulation, legislation, and self-regulation have popped up across the globe.

For example:

- In 2012, Israel passed legislation banning the use of under-weight models in local ads and publications. Models must prove that their BMI exceeds the recommended 18.5.
- "In Italy, Camera Nazionale della Moda Italiana, which orga-nizes the Fashion Weeks in Milan and Rome, agreed to a self-regulation manifesto with the Italian Government. Those signing the manifesto vow not to use models younger than 16 years old and require models to provide medical certificates attesting that they are healthy, based on evaluations devised through the study of eating disorders, including BMI levels. The manifesto states: 'We commit not to use models in shows or photoshoots whose medical certificates prove that they suffer from an eating disorder.'"[3]
- "The organizers of Madrid's Pasarela Cibeles reached a vol-untary agreement with the city's regional government to turn away models with a BMI below 18. Doctors attended the events to check the models. According to the Association of Fashion Designers of Spain, 30% of the models who had pre-viously appeared on the Madrid Fashion Week catwalks were ineligible under the new ruling. However, there is no hard evi-dence about the number of models being banned."[4]
- As for the United States, the Council of Fashion Designers of America (CFDA) has undertaken a self-regulated health initiative, which establishes guidelines for a campaign of awareness and assistance to keep models healthy. "Designers

---

3. *Id.*
4. *Id.*

share a responsibility to protect women, and very young girls in particular, within the business, sending the message that beauty is health. While some models are naturally tall and thin and their appearance is a result of many factors, including genetics, youth, nutritional food, and exercise, other models have or develop eating disorders. Although we cannot fully assume responsibility for an issue that is as complex as eating disorders and that occurs in many walks of life, the fashion industry can begin a campaign of awareness and create an atmosphere that supports the well-being of these young women," notes the CFDA's letter on the health initiative, which was sent out to industry players.[5]

Another area that has received attention in this realm is the retouching of fashion images and advertisements. From famous actresses to ordinary models, companies, magazines, and even Hollywood industries have employed various retouching techniques to make the objects of their pictures seem thinner, taller, more shapely—sometimes to unattainable and impossible proportions.

One author argues that while "[t]hese images all seem harmless, but together they show an epidemic of beauty that is unrealistic and impossible to reach. This has contributed to very real problems of depression, anorexia, bulimia, and other serious health issues among young women. . . . Currently, in the United States alone, nearly ten million women suffer from eating disorders such as anorexia or bulimia."[6]

---

5. Letter to the Industry by Diane von Furstenberg and Steven Kolb on the CFDA Health Initiative (Aug. 22, 2012) (available at http://cfda.com/the-latest/cfda-health-initiative).

6. Kerry C. Donovan, *Vanity Fare: The Cost, Controversy, and Art of Fashion Advertisement Retouching*, 26 Notre Dame J. L. Ethics & Pub Pol'y 583, 607 (2012).

Acknowledging the issue, some governments have attempted to crack down. "The growing use of photoshopping in advertisements coupled with startling statistics regarding female eating disorders has led to the serious contemplation of legislation in countries such as England and France. Meanwhile, Australia recently released voluntary guidelines for the fashion and publishing industries, and the New Zealand government has also started to urge the media to portray women accurately. In other countries, private retailers are taking the initiative themselves and have started 'no retouching' policies."[7]

*"Beauty is how you feel inside, and it reflects in your eyes. It is not something physical."*
— SOPHIA LOREN

Some of the proposed pieces of legislation, the author notes, entail warning labels that would accompany any image that was retouched or photoshopped. In France, for example, one party leader sought to introduce a law that would require a label reading "Photograph retouched to modify the physical appearance of a person," and in Brazil, the required label would read "Attention: image retouched to alter the physical appearance of the person

7.  *Id.* at 583–584.

portrayed."[8] In England, a proposed labeling system for advertisements would not only ban altered images in advertisements aimed at children under the age of sixteen, but also operate as a rating system, under which all advertising photos would be rated on a scale depending on the degree or level of retouching that was used.

Of course, in the United States, regulating photoshopped or retouched advertisements might be problematic, as advertisements are considered commercial speech, which is afforded some protection under the First Amendment and relevant recent decisions of the Supreme Court. As such, images would be scrutinized under the four-pronged *Central Hudson* test, which looks at:

1. whether the ads are deceptive or misleading;

2. whether the government has a legitimate interest in regulating fashion advertisements;

3. whether the regulation directly advances the government's interest; and

4. whether the regulation is not more extensive than necessary to serve the purported governmental interest.[9]

Yet another area in which modeling and the law intersect deals with the use of children as models. In France, strict rules are in place regarding the employment of minors under the age of sixteen, with a specific exception carved out for children employed in the performing arts, advertising, or the fashion industry.[10]

Federal labor laws in the United States likewise regulate the employment of minors under the age of sixteen, imposing bans on hiring minors for certain trades and industries and imposing

---

8. *Id.* at 586.

9. *Id.* at 609–620, citing to *Central Hudson Gas & Elec. v. Pub. Serv. Comm'n of N. Y.*, 447 U.S. 557 (1980).

10. See Benedicte Clin, et al, *Children Employed in the Performing Arts, Advertising, and Fashion Industry: What Legal Protection Do They Have?*, 28 Med & L. 499 (2009).

limitations on when and for how long minors under sixteen may work. According to the Department of Labor:

"Fourteen- and 15-Year-Olds May Not Be Employed:

1. DURING SCHOOL HOURS, *except* as provided in Work Experience and Career Exploration Programs and Work-Study Programs.
2. BEFORE 7 a.m. or AFTER 7 p.m. *except* from June 1 through Labor Day when the evening hour is extended to 9 p.m. (time is based on local standards; i.e., whether the locality has adopted daylight savings time).
3. MORE THAN 3 HOURS A DAY ON A SCHOOL DAY, INCLUDING FRIDAYS.
4. MORE THAN 8 HOURS A DAY ON A NONSCHOOL DAY.
5. MORE THAN 18 HOURS A WEEK DURING A SCHOOL WEEK.
6. MORE THAN 40 HOURS A WEEK DURING NONSCHOOL WEEKS."[11]

In addition, state laws can impose additional rules, such as the requirement of a work permit by minors under a certain age.

There have been efforts to legislate child modeling practices in particular. Versions of the Child Modeling Exploitation Prevention Act were introduced in Congress in 2002 and 2005. The bill would have amended the Fair Labor Standards Act of 1938 to prohibit an employer from employing a child model in exploitive child modeling. It had defined "exploitive child modeling" as "modeling involving the use of a child under 17 years old for financial gain

---

11. Bulletin from the U.S. Dept. of Labor on Child Labor Provisions for Nonagricultural Occupations Under the Fair Labor Standards Act (Feb. 2013) (available at http://www.dol.gov/whd/regs/compliance/childlabor101.pdf).

without the purpose of marketing a product or service other than the child's image, regardless of whether the employment relationship of the child is direct or indirect, contractual or noncontractual, or is termed that of an independent contractor." The bills both died when they were referred to committees.

# Fitness and the Law

*"When real people fall down in life, they get right back up and keep walking."*

**— SARAH JESSICA PARKER, AS CARRIE BRADSHAW IN**
***SEX AND THE CITY***

# Chapter Twenty-Three

# Why Can't I Cancel My Membership?

*Friedman v. 24 Hour Fitness USA, Inc.*, 580 F. Supp. 2d 985 (C.D. Cal. 2008). (class-action litigation)

S ay you've joined a health club. Then say, like many people in the same position, you saw yourself going less and less to work out at said health club. Figuring that your monthly fees can better be put to use, you decide to cancel your membership. Your health club says you will be missed, but lets you out of your monthly contract—only it charges you for "one last month" of membership. Now what recourse do you have?

In 2008, a federal district court in California decided this precise issue. *Friedman v. 24 Hour Fitness USA, Inc.*, dealt with a consumer class-action lawsuit, wherein the plaintiffs claimed their fitness center defrauded them by withdrawing membership fees from their bank and credit card accounts even after the plaintiffs canceled their memberships.[1] In each of the plaintiffs' cases, the defendant fitness center allegedly acknowledged the cancellations

---

1. *Friedman v. 24 Hour Fitness USA, Inc.*, 580 F. Supp. 2d 985 (C.D. Cal. 2008).

of the members' monthly memberships but proceeded to draw at least one additional charge on the plaintiffs' accounts.[2]

The plaintiffs sued under the federal Racketeer Influenced Corrupt Organizations Act (RICO) and the Electronic Funds Transfer Act. They also alleged claims under California state consumer protection statutes, along with claims under California's Unfair Competition Law, based on unfair and fraudulent conduct.[3]

The federal district court largely sided with the plaintiff class. Although the court dismissed the wire fraud claims of five of the six plaintiffs, it allowed the plaintiff class to continue with their claims under RICO[4] and the state Unfair Competition Law, holding that those claims withstood a motion to dismiss.[5]

Some state laws actually regulate health club memberships and contracts. Consider the following example from Illinois:

Contract requirements: cancellation and refund.

a. Every contract for physical fitness services shall provide that:

   1. the contract may be cancelled by the customer within 3 business days after the first business day after the contract is signed by the customer, and that all monies paid pursuant to said contract shall be refunded to the customer. For the purposes of this Section, business day shall mean any day on which the facility is open for business. A customer purchasing a plan at a facility which has not yet opened for business at the time the contract is signed, or who does not purchase a contract at an existing facility, shall have seven calendar days in which to cancel the contract and receive a full refund of all monies

---

2. *Id.* at 989.
3. *Id.* at 988.
4. *Id.* at 993–994.
5. *Id.* at 994–995.

paid. The customer's rights to cancel described herein are in addition to any other contract rights or remedies provided by law;

2. in the event of the relocation of a customer's residence to farther than 25 miles from the center's facilities, and upon the failure of the original center to designate a center, with comparable facilities and services within 25 miles of the customer's new residence, which agrees to accept the original center's obligations under the contract, the customer may cancel the contract and shall be liable for only that portion of the charges allocable to the time before reasonable evidence of such relocation is presented to the center, plus a reasonable fee if so provided in the contract, but such fee shall not exceed 10% of the unused balance, or $50, whichever is less; and

3. if the customer, because of death or disability, is unable to use or receive all services contracted for, the customer, or his estate as the case may be, shall be liable for only that portion of the charges allocable to the time prior to death or the onset of disability. The center shall in such event have the right to require and verify reasonable evidence of such death or disability.

b. Every contract for physical fitness services shall provide that notice of cancellation pursuant to subsection (a) of this Section shall be made in writing and delivered by certified or registered mail to the center at the address specified in the contract. All refunds to which a customer or his estate is entitled shall be made within 30 days of receipt by the center of the cancellation notice.[6]

---

6. 815 ILCS pt. 645 (2012).

# Fashion Law Fact:

According to the Federal Trade Commission, "Weight loss claims must be supported by competent and reliable scientific evidence. Magazine articles, marketing materials from wholesalers, and testimonials from satisfied customers won't do the trick."[7]

---

7. Lesley Fair, *Weighing the Evidence: Substantiating Claims for Weight Loss Products Bureau of Consumer Protection* , BUSINESS.FTC.GOV, http://www.business.ftc. gov/documents/bus09-dietary-supplements-advertising-guide-industry (last visited May 22, 2013).

# Chapter Twenty-Four

# When the Marathon Hurts More Than It Should:

## The Duty of Race Organizers to Provide Adequate Water and Electrolytes

*Saffro v. Elite Racing, Inc.*, 98 Cal. App. 4th 173 (Cal. App. 4th Dist. 2002).

I t's no secret that marathons are extremely treacherous and that running a marathon in the heat can do a number on one's body.

In one case, however, the plaintiff marathon runner claimed it wasn't just the heat but rather the lack of precautions taken by the marathon organizers that caused his injuries. *Saffro v. Elite Racing, Inc.*, centered on the 1998 Suzuki Rock N Roll Marathon, which was put on by the defendant and in which the plaintiff participated.[1]

---

1. *Saffro v. Elite Racing, Inc.* 98 Cal. App. 4th 173 (Cal. App. 4 Dist. 2002).

After the race, the plaintiff boarded a plane to return to his home in Chicago; within sixty to ninety minutes of boarding, he suffered a seizure and had to be hospitalized after an emergency landing. According to the facts of the case, "[h]e was hospitalized in St. Louis and diagnosed with severe hyponatremia—which occurs as a result of decreased sodium concentration in the blood, as well as pulmonary edema and cerebral edema resulting from the hyponatremia. Saffro's condition was critical; he was kept on a ventilator for four days and hospitalized for a longer period. His injuries caused him to suffer neurological deficit; indeed, Saffro's only memory of running the marathon was a "vague recollection of hearing some music, some bands . . . " Saffro submitted the declarations of medical experts who opined that his hyponatremia was caused by the inability to consume adequate amounts of water and fluids containing electrolytes (such as Gatorade and Race Day) during the marathon."

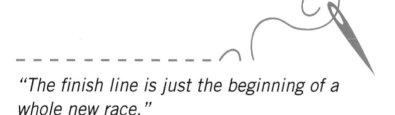

*"The finish line is just the beginning of a whole new race."*

— UNKNOWN

The plaintiff sued the race organizers in a California court for negligence and negligent supervision, claiming that the marathon organizers failed to provide adequate fluids along the course route.

He lost in the trial court when the court granted summary judgment for the race organizers.

On appeal, however, the court overturned the district court's decision and held that the organizers had a duty to produce a reasonably safe event and minimize the risks of the event without altering the nature of the sport.[2] "This duty includes the obligation to minimize the risks of dehydration and hyponatremia by providing adequate water and electrolyte fluids along the 26-mile course—particularly where the race organizer represents to the participants that these will be available at specific locations throughout the race."[3]

---

2. *Id.* at 179.
3. *Id.*

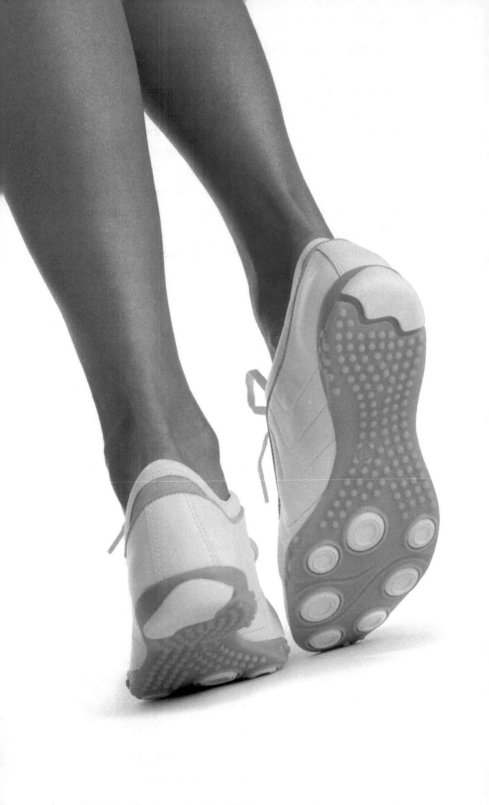

# Chapter Twenty-Five

# Race to the Trademark

*Boston Athletic Ass'n v. Sullivan*, 867 F.2d 22 (1st Cir. 1989).

Fashion and athletics often go together, and sponsorships of athletic apparel, sports logos, and other related items are often big business.

In one case, the Boston Athletic Association (BAA), which notably sponsors the Boston Marathon, brought suit against a retailer of athletic equipment, seeking to enjoin the retailer from manufacturing and selling unlicensed T-shirts that bore the Boston Marathon logo. The district court denied the injunction, but on appeal, the First Circuit Court of Appeals reversed.

"There is no genuine issue of fact with respect to the likelihood of confusion of goods. Nor is there any genuine issue of fact that the purchasing public will likely believe that the sponsor of the Boston Marathon produces, licenses or otherwise endorses defendants' shirts and other goods with logos referring to the Boston Marathon. . . .[1] The plaintiff, BAA, owns the name 'Boston Marathon' and the defendants' shirts imprinted with logos suggesting

---

1. *Boston Athletic Ass'n v. Sullivan*, 867 F.2d 22, 35 (1st Cir.1989).

167

that event constitute an infringement of BAA's mark."[2] By using the marathon logo, the defendant was liable for its infringement.

Of course, athletic apparel cases continue to see the light of day in courts. In a recent decision, the U.S. Supreme Court addressed Nike's "Air Force 1" trademark, after Nike filed suit against a smaller retailer, Already LLC, alleging that the defendant infringed on Nike's trademark in its manufacturing and selling shoes with a similar design. Already LLC counterclaimed, disputing the validity of the Air Force 1 trademark.[3]

While the initial suit was pending, Nike issued a covenant not to sue, whereby it promised not to raise any infringement claims against Already LLC for its existing shoe designs or any "colorable imitations" of Nike's designs that may occur in the future. Nike then dropped its claim against Already LLC and asked the district court to dismiss Already's counterclaim.[4]

The court granted Nike's request, but Already (after unsuccessfully opposing the motion) appealed, claiming the following:

- that Nike did not prove that the original claims were moot simply because the covenant not to sue was in effect, as Already planned to introduce other lines of shoes that the Covenant may not cover;
- that investors would not invest in Already's line of shoes until Nike's trademark was invalidated; and
- that Nike intimidated retailers into refusing to carry Already's shoes.[5]

---

2. *Id.*
3. *Already, LLC v. Nike, Inc.*, No. 11-982 (U.S. Jan. 9, 2013).
4. *Id.*
5. *Id.*

The Second Circuit Court, and ultimately the Supreme Court, both affirmed the dismissal of Already's claim, holding that the case was moot and that Nike's covenant not to sue was sufficiently broad to apply to Already's future designs.[6]

# Fashion Law Fact:

Under revised Federal Trade Commission guidelines, "advertisements that feature a consumer and convey his or her experience with a product or service as typical when that is not the case will be required to clearly disclose the results that consumers can generally expect. . . . [M]aterial connections (sometimes payments or free products) between advertisers and endorsers—connections that consumers would not expect—must be disclosed."[7]

6. *Id.*
7. News Release, Federal Trade Commission, FTC Publishes Final Guides Governing Endorsements, Testimonials (Oct. 5, 2009) (available at http://www.ftc.gov/opa/2009/10/endortest.shtm).

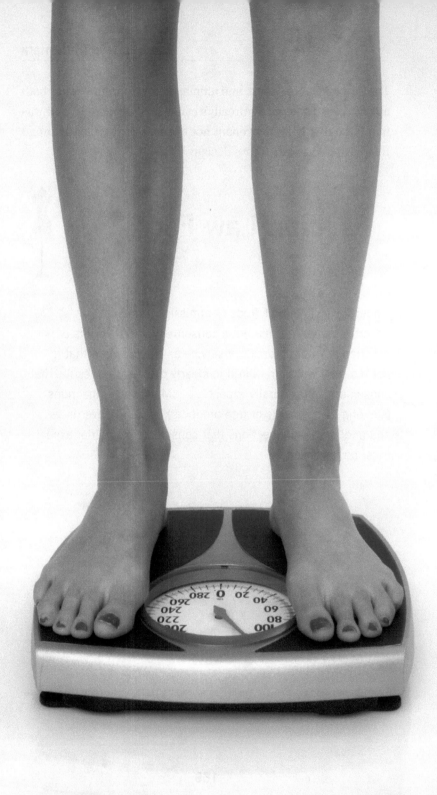

# Chapter Twenty-Six

# When That Diet Does Not Work as Promised:

## FTC Probes into Companies' Claims and Ensuing Class-Action Litigation by Consumers

**D**iet pills are not food, nor are they drugs per se—most qualify as nutritional supplements, and it is a known issue that those supplements do not receive the same rigorous regulations as, say, a food product or medicine would.

Still, the makers of diet pills surely cannot claim miraculous results falsely, right? The Federal Trade Commission (FTC) has indeed probed into diet companies' claims, and some class-action litigation by consumers has ensued.

In fact, the FTC's list of advertising cases involving weight loss products and services dates back to 1927![1] Consider the following examples:

---

1. News Release, Federal Trade Commission, Federal Trade Commission Advertising Cases Involving Weight Loss Products and Services 1927–May 2003 (available at http://www.ftc.gov/opa/1997/03/dietcase.shtm).

- *Slim Down Solution, LLC, and MaderiaManagement, Inc.*, involved a complaint for permanent injunction and alleged false and unsubstantiated claims for a purported weight loss product containing D-glucosamine.[2]
- *Nutri/System, Inc.*, resulting in a consent order, involved "claims that scientific studies show that users of its low calorie program customers lose at least 29 % more weight than dieters on other programs; customers reach weight loss goals within certain predicted time frames; program complies with American Medical Association, American Heart Association, and American Dietetic Association guidelines, and Healthline magazine evaluations and ratings; and is approved by Stanford University."[3]
- *Weight Watchers International, Inc.*, also resulting in a consent order, involved claims that the company's low-calorie diet program was superior to others.[4]
- *Jenny Craig, Inc.*, involved "claims that customers of low-calorie weight loss programs reach weight loss goals within certain predicted time frames" and resulted in a consent order.[5]

The FTC's authority to regulate these advertisements lies mainly in two sources: the FTC's Deception Policy Statement and its Standard for Substantiation of Health Claims.[6]

---

2. *Slim Down Solution, LLC, and Maderia Management, Inc.*, Civ. Action No. 03-80051-CIV-PAINE (S.D. Fla.).

3. *See supra* note 282, citing to *Nutri/System, Inc.*, 116 F.T.C. 1408 (1993).

4. *Weight Watchers International, Inc.*, Docket No. 9261, 1997 FTC Lexis 360 (Dec. 24, 1997).

5. *See supra* note 282, citing to *Jenny Craig, Inc.*, 125 F.T.C. 333 (Feb. 19, 1998).

6. Enforcement Policy Statement from Federal Trade Commission on Food Advertising (May 1994) (available at http://www.ftc.gov/bcp/policystmt/ad-food.shtm).

"As set out in the Deception Statement, the Commission will find an advertisement deceptive under Section 5 and, therefore, unlawful, if it contains a representation or omission of fact that is likely to mislead consumers acting reasonably under the circumstances, and that representation or omission is material."[7]

The Standard for Substantiation of Health Claims is "based on the totality of the publicly available scientific evidence (including evidence from well-designed studies conducted in a manner that is consistent with generally recognized scientific procedures and principles), that there is significant scientific agreement, among experts qualified by scientific training and experience to evaluate such claims, that the claim is supported by such evidence."[8]

# Fashion Law Fact:

Diets are big business. The diet industry grosses over $33 billion annually.[9]

---

7. *Id.*

8. *Id.*

9. Kerry C. Donovan, *Vanity Fare: The Cost, Controversy, and Art of Fashion Advertisement Retouching*, 26 NOTRE DAME J. L. ETHICS & PUB POL'Y 581, 607 (2012).

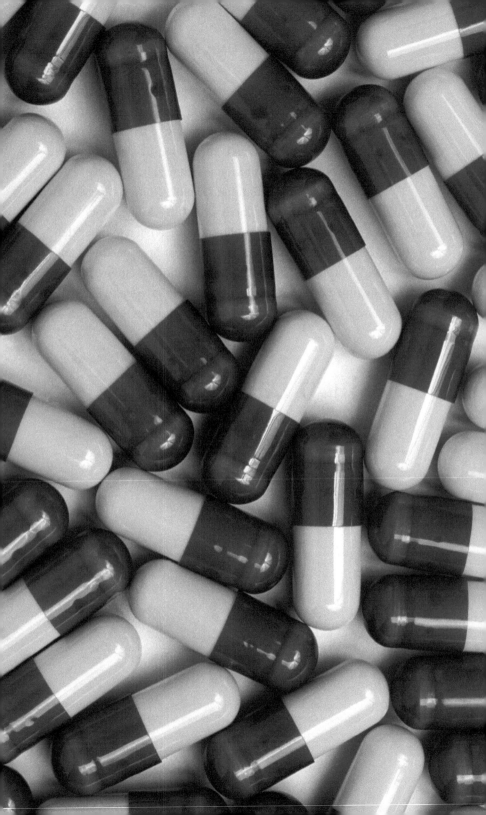

# Chapter Twenty-Seven

# When Beauty Hurts:
## Blockbuster Lawsuits Involving Diet and Beauty Products

Fen-Phen Litigation.

Breast Implant Litigation.

O nce upon a time, women opted to undergo surgery to have silicone-filled sacks implanted into their bodies, for the sake of making their breasts appear larger or shapelier. We now know this is not a great idea, of course, and we have a long list of cases, regulations, and research to support it. The first silicone breast implants were developed in the 1960s.[1] The first suit against a silicone breast manufacturer developed in the following decade. The following are some of the highlights of ensuing litigation and regulations:

- The first lawsuit against Dow Corning took place in 1977; it was brought by a Cleveland woman who claimed that her ruptured implants and ensuing surgeries caused her pain and suffering. The suit was settled for $170,000.[2]

---

1. *Breast Implants on Trial*, PBS.ORG, http://www.pbs.org/wgbh/pages/frontline/implants/cron.html (last visited May 22, 2013).
2. *Id.*

- In 1984, in *Stern v. Dow Corning Corp.*, a California plaintiff recovered $211,000 in compensatory damages and $1.5 in punitive damages after successfully arguing that her autoimmune disease resulted from her silicone breast implants.[3]
- In 1991, in *Toole v. Baxter Corp.*, an Alabama plaintiff recovered $5.4 million after showing preliminary symptoms of systemic autoimmune problems and her doctors found silicone in her lymphatic system. The federal circuit court, on appeal by the manufacturer, affirmed the lower court decision in 2000.[4]
- Also in 1991, in *Hopkins v. Dow Corning Corp.*, a California woman recovered $7.3 million. Her connective-tissue disease was linked to her ruptured silicone breast implants. Once again, the federal circuit court affirmed the verdict on appeal.[5]
- The first class-action suit was filed in February 1992. By the end of that year, over 12,000 suits had been filed against Dow Corning.[6]
- In March 1994, "[t]he class action suit is finalized by manufacturers with Dow Corning being the largest contributor. The other contributors include Baxter, Bristol-Myers Squibb/MEC, [and] 3M. It is the largest class-action settlement in history. Manufacturers claim there is no scientific evidence linking silicone breast implants with autoimmune diseases. There are set monetary amounts that will be awarded to women with specific medical conditions. No requirements are needed to prove implants are the cause of their ailments. Women will be allowed to drop out of the settlement. Companies can

3. *Stern v. Dow Corning Corp.*, No. C-83-2348-MMP (N.D. Cal. 1985).
4. *Toole v. Baxter Health Corp.*, 235 F.3d 1307 (11th Cir. 2000).
5. *Hopkins v. Dow Corning Corp.*, 33 F.3d 1116 (9th Cir. 1994).
6. *See supra* note 292.

also opt out if too few women register claims."[7] By the next year, nearly half a million women had registered in the global settlement.[8]

*"Fashion is very important. It is life-enhancing, and like everything that gives pleasure, it is worth doing well."*

**—VIVIENNE WESTWOOD**

Cases and settlements regarding silicone breast implants continued well into the late 1990s. But it didn't take long for the large breast implant settlement to be beat by another figure—this one centering on a diet drug.

Remember Fen-Phen? Short for fenfluramine and phentermine, the two drugs that made up the diet pill, it was prescribed to as many as 18 million people, according to the New York Times. The drug was pulled off the shelves by the Food and Drug Administration in 1997, after it was linked to heart valve defects. Lawsuits ensued against the drug's makers and sellers, and in 1999, American Home Products, the manufacturer of the drug, agreed to a blockbuster settlement in the amount of $3.75 billion.

---

7. *Id.*
8. *Id.*

# Index

# Index

# Index

# Index

# About the Author

Ursula Furi-Perry is the author of nine other books: *50 Legal Careers for Non-Attorneys* (ABA Publishing 2008); *50 Unique Legal Paths: How to Find the Right Job* (ABA Publishing 2008); *Law School Revealed: Secrets, Opportunities and Success!* (Jist Publishing May 2009); *Trial Prep for Paralegals* (National Institute for Trial Advocacy 2009) (coauthor); *Your First Year As a Lawyer Revealed* (Jist Publishing 2010); *The Legal Assistant's Complete Desk Reference* (ABA Publishing 2011 and 2013); *Trial Prep for the New Advocate* (LexisNexis via National Institute for Trial Advocacy 2011) (coauthor); *The Millennial Lawyer: Making the Most of Generational Differences in the Firm* (ABA Publishing 2012); and *Constitutional Law for Kids* (ABA Publishing 2013). Furi-Perry has also published more than three hundred articles in national and regional publications, including Law.com, American Lawyer Media, *Legal Assistant Today*, *Pre-Law Magazine*, *National Jurist*, and LawCrossing.com.

Furi-Perry is director of Academic Support and director of Bar Essay Writing at the Massachusetts School of Law at Andover. She received her juris doctor, magna cum laude, from the Massachusetts School of Law. She is a partner in the firm of Dill & Furi-Perry, LLP, in Haverhill, Massachusetts.